EUGENE ESMONDE
VC, DSO

Chaz Bowyer

WILLIAM KIMBER · LONDON

First published in 1983 by
WILLIAM KIMBER & CO. LIMITED
100 Jermyn Street, London, SW1Y 6EE

© Chaz Bowyer, 1983

ISBN 0-7183-0409-8

Photoset in North Wales by
Derek Doyle & Associates, Mold, Clwyd
and Printed in Great Britain by
Redwood Burn, Trowbridge

Dedication

Went the day well?
We died and never knew
But, well or ill, Freedom
We died for you.

Anon

Contents

List of Illustrations

Introduction

Duty is defined in dictionaries as ' ... that which is demanded by law, morality, social conscience, a moral obligation'; while Wordsworth termed duty the 'stern daughter of the voice of God'. The armed Services of all countries lay down basic standards of duty, i.e. rules and regulations defining precisely the minimum standards of conduct expected from their members in almost every circumstance. Yet none specify that epitome of devotion to duty exemplified by countless Servicemen and women – ultimate self-sacrifice in the pursuit of what each considered his or her true duty. Such selflessness can only spring from an inner conviction or faith; a pure life-or-death decision which can never be fully imposed by any higher authority. Any such decision means a man must first overcome the primeval instinct of self-preservation – survival – then deliberately plunge into a situation from which there can be no return.

One of the many men faced with such a decision during the 1939-45 war was Eugene Esmonde. In 1940, in a letter to his home in Ireland, Esmonde had written, 'I can think of no greater honour, nor a better way of passing into Eternity than in the cause for which the Allies are fighting this war.' Some two years later Esmonde died in an action still regarded by many as possibly a supreme example of raw courage, and a superlative demonstration of all that is implied by 'devotion to duty'. It was a selfless sacrifice made all the more poignant when it is remembered that, being Irish-born, he might easily have remained a neutral throughout the war.

No biography can truly claim to be absolutely complete; every man's life inevitably contains myriad facets which are impossible to account in mere print, while any man's inner thoughts and reasoning are essentially hidden from the onlooker. There is too the question of essential documents and records relating to any particular subject, many of these all too often being lost to posterity and thereby creating minor gaps in chronology *et al*. Such appears to be the case of Eugene Esmonde. For example, despite exhaustive research over many years, the location (if any) of Esmonde's various flying log books of his service with the RAF, Imperial Airways, and Fleet Air Arm is still elusive; while certain contemporary official or demi-official papers relating to the fated Allied air operations on 12 February 1942 are (apparently) 'missing' from the available archives. Thus, this book must be regarded as primarily a belated tribute to the extraordinary courage of an unquestionably brave and rare man.

One final apology is offered to readers of a former book of mine, *For Valour – The Air VCs* (Kimber, 1978), in which I incorrectly attributed to Eugene Esmonde a second Christian name 'Kingsmill', due to my acceptance in all good faith of an ostensibly authentic document which has since been confirmed as non-authentic. The path to truth is demonstrably a rocky road indeed for those who care for such matters.

Chaz Bowyer
Norwich, 1983

CHAPTER ONE

Roots

Eugene Esmonde's first breath was drawn at four o'clock in the wintry morning of 1 March 1909 – and was almost his last. The elder by mere minutes of twin sons born to Eily Josephine Esmonde, wife of a medical general practitioner, Dr John Joseph Esmonde, Eugene and his twin James Bartholomew weighed scarcely six pounds between them, and neither boy was expected to live long. Indeed, James had been laid aside initially as already dead when his father picked up the frail little body, saying, 'Give the poor little chap a chance', then proceeded to slap enough vigour into it to start James breathing. Eugene, after some anxious moments for his parents, gave ample evidence that he would survive without the need for such violent treatment. The place was Huthwaite House in the Yorkshire mining village of Thurgoland, near Sheffield, where Dr Esmonde had his contemporary practice, and at the moment of birth a snowstorm was raging outside. Thus Eugene became the fourth son born to Eily Esmonde; the latest member of a family capable of tracing its ancestry back to the Normans ten centuries before.

The Esmonde lineage had its constant firm roots in Ireland (now Eire), a succession of highly individual men and women, once described by one historian as 'More Irish than the Irish'. The family seat, virtually from the tenth century, was in Wexford, mainly descending from Henry Esmonde, Senechal of Wexford in 1294, with one member, John, becoming Bishop of Ferns in 1340. By the reign of Elizabeth I of England the head of the house was Sir Laurence Esmonde (1570?-1646) who abandoned the traditional Roman Catholic creed of his forebears and professed himself a Protestant, then took up arms in the service of the Virgin Queen. During one of his armed expeditions into Connaught he fell in love with Margaret O'Flaherty, daughter of the Dynast of Iar (Connaught), whom he married and who bore him a son, Thomas. A lady who was as remarkable for her orthodoxy as for her considerable personal charms, Margaret feared lest her son might be raised as a Protestant and consequently fled with the boy to her family in Connaught. Laurence Esmonde promptly repudiated her, on the plea that a marriage between a Catholic and a Protestant was voidable in law. He next married Elizabeth Butler, grand-daughter of James, ninth Earl of Ormonde.

In December 1606 Sir Laurence became governor of the important fort of Duncannon, a post he was to retain until the year of his death; while some six years later he was given a grant of 1500 acres of confiscated lands as a reward for his services to the English Crown. In 1619 he purchased more lands in Wicklow, albeit in highly dubious circumstances, and by 1622 owned large properties in Wexford, Waterford, Kilkenny and Tipperary. In the same year, on 20 May, he was raised to the peerage as Lord Esmonde, Baron of Limbrick, County Wexford. In the late summer of 1646 Laurence died and was buried at Limerick in the grounds of a church he had himself built. Not having any children from his second marriage, he bequeathed his vast properties to Thomas Esmonde, son of his first wife Margaret.

This son, Thomas, soon followed the fighting traditions of the Esmondes by serving in the armies of the King of Sweden, and later commanded a regiment in the siege of La Rochelle, then raised a troop of horse for the service of King Charles I of England. His reward for the latter support was his creation as a baronet in 1628, only to be attainted by the Cromwellian Parliament in 1642 and have his estates confiscated. Nevertheless, Thomas's son Laurence became the second Baronet Esmonde and served in the French Army before being created a Privy Councillor by King James II. Of his descendants, one Maurice saw active service with the Austrian Army and attained the rank of Baron; while Maurice's daughter married a Count Kavanagh. The fifth baronet, Sir John Esmonde, served in the Spanish Army, and took part in the 1736 siege of Naples; while Sir James Esmonde (seventh Baronet) and his son Sir Thomas Esmonde (eighth Baronet) both served with the French Army.

Not all male Esmondes sought army careers, however. One John Esmonde was hanged by the British in 1798, yet his son later joined the English Navy and eventually captained a frigate named *Lion*, the first ship to bear that title. The ninth Baronet (of Ballystranagh) had three sons – John (later tenth Baronet), James, and the youngest, Thomas. Young Thomas pursued an Army career, joining the 18th Royal Irish Regiment on leaving school in November 1851, in the rank of Ensign, and seeing fighting service in India and the 1852-53 Burmese campaign. Promoted to Lieutenant in June 1853, Thomas moved with his regiment to take part in the Crimean War, 1854-55, being present at the siege of Sebastopol (December 1854 to July 1855), including the well-known assault on the Cemetery on the fortieth anniversary of the battle of Waterloo. For his personal bravery on 18 and 20 June 1855 Thomas Esmonde, by then a Captain, was subsequently awarded a Victoria Cross (gazetted 25 September 1857) the citation for which read:

For having, after being engaged in the attack on the Redan, repeatedly assisted at great personal risk, under a heavy fire of shell and grape, in rescuing wounded men from exposed situations; and also, while in command of a covering party two days later, after having rushed it with the most prompt and daring gallantry to the spot where a fireball from the enemy had just lodged, which he effectually extinguished before it had betrayed the position of the working party under his protection, thus saving it from a murderous fire of shell and grape which was immediately opened upon the spot where the fireball had fallen.

In December 1857 Thomas Esmonde VC was promoted to Major, and in November of the following year married Matilda O'Kelly. Becoming Lieutenant-Colonel and ADC to the Lord Lieutenant of Ireland on 2 December 1868, Thomas retired from the army on that date by the sale of his commission. His next appointment was as Deputy Inspector-General of the Royal Irish Constabulary, but when riding with the Kildares one day in 1872 he was struck in one eye severely by a branch as he cleared a thorn fence. The eye became badly inflamed, his other eye soon became affected, brain fever followed, and on 14 January 1873, in Bruges, Belgium, Thomas Esmonde VC died. Of his five children, his only son, Thomas Louis Esmonde, was drowned in 1917 when the cross-Channel steamer he was travelling on was sunk by a German submarine.

Of Thomas Esmonde VC's two brothers, John (tenth Baronet) was succeeded by a son, also named Thomas, as the eleventh Baronet at the tender age of nine years. Accordingly, the other brother, James, became legal guardian of the boy and lived in the ancient family home of Ballystranagh, County Wexford until the eleventh Baronet came of age. James then married and set up his own home, buying a handsome Georgian mansion, Drominagh, set high above the shore of Lough Derg on the River Shannon in Tipperary, together with some 600 acres of lush farmland. Once settled in the new home James Esmonde fathered three sons, namely James, John Joseph, and Richard. The younger James died in 1897 without issue, while Richard died in infancy. John Joseph, however, married Rose McGuinness who bore him three sons and three daughters before her premature death. John Joseph remarried, this time to Eily Josephine O'Sullivan of the Bere O'Sullivans, by whom he was to father a further six boys and a girl; these, in birthdate sequence, being Owen, Donal, John Witham, Eugene (the subject of this book) and James Bartholomew, Carmel, and Patrick; the eldest boy, Owen, being born on 15 May 1905. As a medical doctor John Joseph based his large family wherever his current practice happened to be – e.g. Owen had been born in London, but by 1909 he was a GP at Thurgoland, Yorkshire where Eugene and his twin James were ushered into the world. In that year, however, John Joseph inherited Drominagh and therefore returned with his family to Ireland to take up occupation of what was to be the Esmonde home for four generations.

Fiercely Irish-Catholic, with a gift for oratory, and a committed nationalist who constantly consigned all matters British to perdition, John Joseph Esmonde gave up his medical practice in 1910 to enter the political arena, being elected MP for Tipperary (North Riding) as one of the famed John Redmond's Home Rule Party. Yet, with characteristic 'Irish' contradiction, when the war between Britain and Germany erupted in 1914, John Joseph

Colonel Thomas Esmonde, VC.

(Right) Dr John Esmonde and his fiancée Eily O'Sullivan, 1904.

(Below) Dr John Esmonde, MD, MP (left) with Joe Devlin, MP, circa 1912.

immediately enlisted in the Royal Army Medical Corps (RAMC), being commissioned as a captain, and being appointed medical officer to the Garrison Barracks in Templemore. Shortly after taking up this appointment, however, he contracted a mild illness and returned to Drominagh to convalesce, only to die in April 1915, aged fifty-three, from an unheralded heart attack.

His sudden death immediately created something of a legal problem, inasmuch as the Drominagh property was left in trust to all the children of his first marriage – through whom, incidentally, the baronetcy line also descended – and the only practical solution was for Drominagh to be sold, and the proceeds therefrom distributed appropriately. John Joseph Esmonde, though a devoted father and husband, had not been a particularly provident man, nor had his medical practice been any basis for prosperity. Fortunately, Eily Esmonde's family were relatively well placed to provide her with sufficient funds to purchase Drominagh and some 300 acres of its land. The money thus raised from the sale, and the sale of the remaining 300 acres, enabled the completion of the education of the children of Rose Esmonde née McGuinness, leaving Eily and her seven children in full residence of the family home.

Also fortunate, at least initially, was the fact that Eily Esmonde had a modest income from a family trust fund which, added to the relatively good contemporary return from farming produce, offered some relief for a widow with seven very small offspring to raise and educate, the eldest, Owen, being not yet ten years of age. If the immediate future seemed bleak for Eily Esmonde, she mustered all the courage, faith, and determination of her forebears and faced that future squarely.

CHAPTER TWO

Adolescence

While the financial problems for Eily Esmonde in raising and educating a large, very young family, added to the maintenance of a large house and its farming, were to be daunting and ever-present, the children – in the main unconscious of any such adult matters – grew up in truly splendid surroundings in the context of natural beauty. The family house Drominagh was situated on a high promontory running out into Lough Derg (a lake of some 200 square miles), with breathtaking vistas of the mountains of Clare and Arra to the west and south, the Slieve Bloom mountains to the east, and the Devil's Bit and Keeper Hill to the south-east; views stretching to fifty miles in certain directions.

Surrounding the property was some of the richest, unspoilt country life it was possible to find in any part of Ireland. On the rock by the shore stood the old keep of the O'Kennedys, from the top of which the whole great lake in summer shimmered in dancing sunlit wavelets at its feet. The lake provided sailing, rowing, fishing and safe swimming in virtually all weathers, while great gaggles of duck and wild geese, sometimes a snow-white armada of swans, came in to shore across the ever-changing colours of the water. Around the lake shores and inland bogs wild life abounded in profusion – all in all, an unequalled, magnificent playground for the Esmonde family to enjoy and use at will.

Being of such tender years, the younger boys were unaffected by their father's death, but the oldest, Owen, now had the mantle of 'man of the house' thrust upon his small shoulders; a duty he was given on the day of the bereavement by being told to take Eugene and his twin brother James to walk up and down sedately on the front lawn in order to spare them the sad atmosphere within the house. Barely five years old, the twins' perfectly natural inclination for fun and games had to be restrained by Owen lest the adults

Eily Esmonde with her first son, Owen, 1905.

looked askance at such frivolities in the circumstances.

Over the following years Eily's seven offspring tended to fall naturally into three groups, with Owen, Donal and Witham under the eagle eye of a strict governess, Eugene and James in the care of a nursery governess, and the babies Carmel and Patrick ('Paddy') in the nursery. Consequently each group had relatively small contact with the others in the daily family round.

As twins, Eugene and James ('Jimmy') were both of small stature from the outset; indeed, neither were to grow taller than five feet and eight inches in manhood. In most other ways, however, it would be difficult to imagine more dissimilar twins. Whereas James was fairish of hair and general appearance and very much the extrovert, Eugene had inherited the near-black hair and sallow complexion of the O'Sullivans via his mother, and was an introvert; a serious boy, deep-thinking, yet with a puckish sense of humour which he retained throughout his lifetime.

Never one to push himself forward, Eugene tended to appear shy and retiring in company, though his somewhat swarthy appearance often attracted attention, as on one occasion when Eily accompanied her children to a fancy dress dance in nearby Nenagh, the county town. Another mother sitting beside Eily asked quite innocently, 'Who is that beautiful little girl over there?' Eily replied, 'That beautiful little girl happens to be my fourth son !'

Growing up in such lush natural surroundings the Esmonde children quickly absorbed and delighted in the myriad ways of nature and wildlife, particularly under the aegis of Danny Donohoe, steward and gardener at the ripe old age of eighty years, whose encyclopaedic knowledge of trees and plants was only matched by his son Jack's equal acquaintance with the ways of birds and animal life and lore. Jack, who had served during the Great War of 1914-18 in the same regiment as Eugene's great-uncle, Thomas Esmonde, VC, had lost a leg on active service, but his physical activities appeared undiminished. From these and their own observations and investigations Eugene and his brothers accumulated a deep love, knowledge and respect of nature.

In 1916 Owen was sent to Downside Abbey in Somerset to commence his academic education, being joined there in the following year by Donal and Witham, and their former governess

(Right) Donal Esmonde, shortly after his ordination, 1932.

(Below) Drominagh – the Esmonde family home.

took over charge of Eugene and James. A strict disciplinarian of the old school, her reign over the energetic twins was to be relatively brief, with the governess finally complaining that she had not taken charge of them early enough to be able to influence their behaviour or attitudes to authority.

As the twins neared the age for them to attend formal schooling, Eily Esmonde decided to take a house in the London area in order to send the boys as day boarders to the Jesuit College at Wimbledon. This move was made in 1919 and the arrangement was to last until 1923, though the long summer vacations were spent back at Drominagh each year. It was while resident in London that Eugene displayed in a minor way a characteristic part of his inner strength of will. On a bicycle trip to visit friends in Surbiton, Eugene's vehicle became trapped in some tramlines, catapulting him under the hooves and wheels of a following pony and trap. He sustained a broken wrist, yet bore the pain stoically and without a murmur of complaint.

By 1923 the general family situation had changed. Owen by then was back in Ireland, commuting daily from Drominagh on a second-hand BSA motor-cycle over the seventeen miles to his latest appointment as a junior bank clerk with the Nenagh branch of the National Bank; while Donal had joined the Mill Hill Society of Missionary Fathers as a clerical student, and Witham was studying for an entrance examination to the Royal Navy. Eily Esmonde therefore decided to give up the Wimbledon house and move back permanently to Drominagh with her remaining children.

On their return to Ireland Eugene and James initially attended the Clongowes Wood College, but this arrangement ceased after only a few terms when Eugene announced that he wished to follow his older brother Donal's example by joining the Mill Hill Fathers, with a view to becoming a foreign missionary eventually. James was therefore brought home for private tutoring. Eugene, accordingly, joined the Mill Hill Fathers at St Peter's College at Freshfield, Lancashire and spent two years there before transferring to Burn Hall in County Durham for a third year of study.

Throughout those three years Eugene invariably spent his few holidays at Drominagh – such was his deep love for his mother, family, and home – where, depending on whom of the many

Eugene Esmonde in the grounds of *Drominagh*, 1925.

(Left) Captain John Witham Esmonde, RN, who died on 28 March, 1983 *(Right)* Eily Esmonde on *Drominagh*'s front lawn, circa 1930.

(Below) James Esmonde, Eugene's twin, circa 1968. James became a polio victim for some 20 years before his death on 9 May 1970.

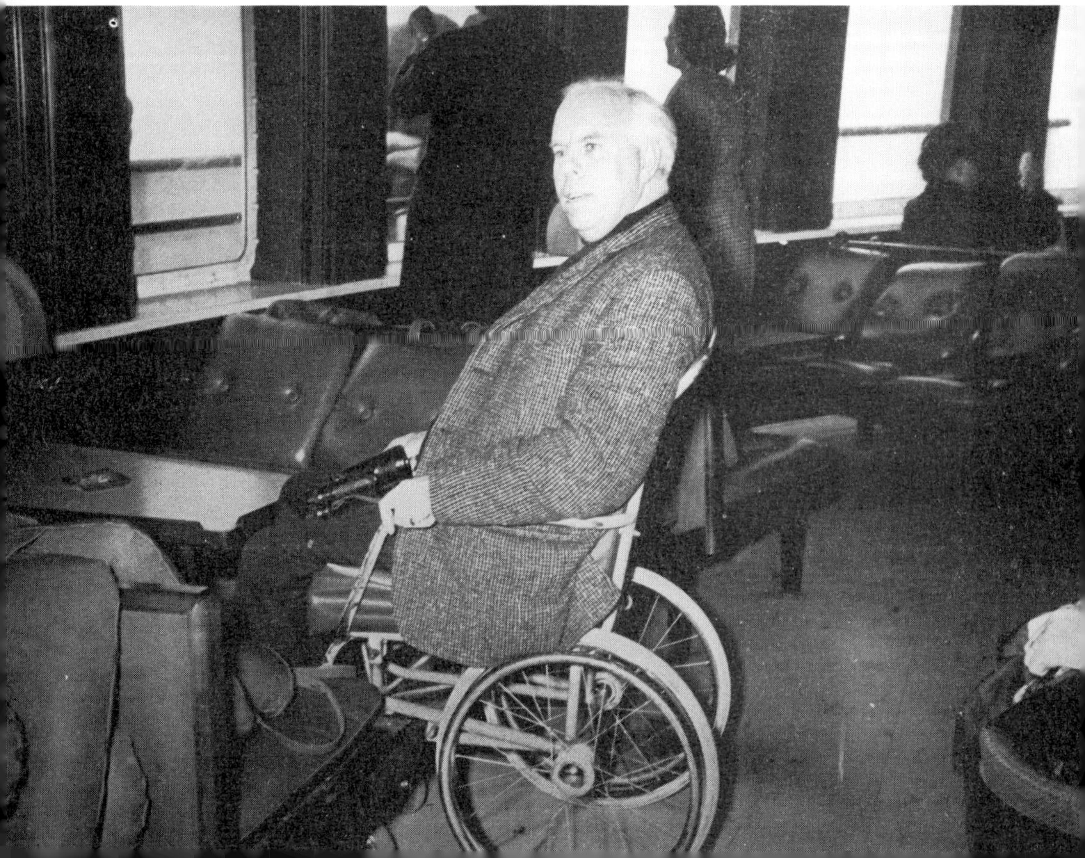

children were holidaying in the house at the same time, he joined his brothers in shooting, fishing, sailing and swimming expeditions. Unlike his brothers, Eugene was by no means an accomplished horseman, though his lack of expertise did not deter him from occasionally joining any family riding outing, albeit often resulting in being unseated.

Though an extremely happy period in many ways for the Esmondes, the same years brought a steady decline in the financial fortunes of Drominagh. Owen, after one year at the Nenagh bank, left his clerk's desk and returned to the family home to take up farming under the skilled tutelage of Danny Donohoe, the farm steward, but the World War boom in farming prices was now ending with a consequential lowering of profit margins for farm produce. In addition world markets were about to slump into a devastating depression, and an economic 'war' with Britain was on the brink. Against this gloomy backdrop Drominagh, at least for the moment, continued to be the venue for each of the Esmonde children whenever their respective life-styles permitted, and the tall grey house witnessed many dances, balls, hunt meets and other gaieties during the mid-1930s.

In the same period Eugene, while applying himself wholeheartedly to his ambition to become a missionary, had begun to have doubts as to his true vocation. Finally, after several sessions of consulting his spiritual director, he decided that the priesthood was not to be his future and, albeit with some reluctance, he gave up his studies and returned to the peace and quiet of Drominagh to rationalise his thoughts. Whether Eugene's doubts were fully justified in this context is now a moot point.

A fellow student who later became a missionary said of him, 'His contemporaries, both among the students and the staff, have an outstanding remembrance of his wonderful charm of character and his considerate gentle ways, so very exceptional for a boy of his age. He had the makings of a great missionary and we were all very sorry when he left us.'

Eugene's decision had no basis in doubt of his firmly held creed of Catholicism – he was to remain wholly inculcated with his faith until his death – but simply exemplified his characteristic constant need to be totally absorbed in any project undertaken.

Nevertheless, the decision left Eugene terribly depressed and troubled on first returning to Ireland, a state of mind exacerbated by the fact that he had fallen deeply in love with a 21-year-old girl who ultimately confessed she did not return his love. This rejection frankly distressed Eugene and, though he continued to enjoy female companionship in general throughout his remaining years, it is the opinion of those closest to him that his love for this girl remained unwavering until the end.

Once his initial moods of depression had lessened, however, Eugene cast around for some profession or career which might offer not only some form of security but especially opportunities for foreign travel; the latter urge being an instinctive restlessness inherited from the Esmonde blood-line through the ages. It was then that he saw an advertisement by the Air Ministry in London offering suitably qualified applicants a Short Service Commission in the Royal Air Force as pilots for five years' active, followed by four years' reserve service, with a possibility of eventual consideration for a permanent commission in the Service. The prospect appealed greatly to Eugene and he duly applied. In due course he was notified of his acceptance, on probation, and commenced his RAF service on 28 December 1928.

CHAPTER THREE

Wings

Eugene Esmonde reported to No 2 Flying Training School at Digby, Lincolnshire on 13 January 1929 as an Acting Pilot Officer (on probation) to commence his pilot training. At that time No 2 FTS had a motley mixture of Vickers Vimy bombers, Bristol F2bs, De Havilland 9As, and Avro 504Ns for instructional purposes, and it was on the latter type, the Avro 504N 'Lynx' two-seater, that Esmonde began his tuition; this *ab initio* phase lasting some five months, under the aegis of the Chief Instructor, Squadron Leader (later, Air Commodore, OBE) R.D. Oxland. Esmonde proved to be a 'natural' pilot, adapting easily to the new element and seemingly revelling in his chosen career. By July that year he and his fellow-entry pupils moved on to the senior term phase, flying the heavier (and trickier) DH9As and Bristol F2bs, and Esmonde finally received his RAF pilot's wings on 13 December 1929.

His first posting after training was to No 26 (Army Co-operation) Squadron at Catterick, Yorkshire. This unit, which had reformed at Catterick on 11 October 1927, was commanded by Squadron Leader R.L. Stevenson MBE, and was equipped with Armstrong Whitworth Atlas aircraft. Esmonde was allocated to A Flight and soon became immersed in the daily routine of a unit tasked with the myriad requirements of close tactical co-operation with various Army formations. As always, he was quiet and unassuming in his relations with other squadron personnel, but spent much of his off-duty hours studying hard for his ultimate ambition – a permanent commission in the RAF. In this he was encouraged by his Flight commander, Flight Lieutenant (later Group Captain) F.W.H. Hall.

However, his service with 26 Squadron was relatively brief, and on 3 March 1930 he was posted to No 43 Squadron based at Tangmere, Sussex. This posting was virtually a compliment to

Avro 504N 'Lynx' trainer, J8982.

Student pilots at No. 2 FTS, Digby, Spring 1929. Eugene Esmonde is fourth from left, seated.

Esmonde's capabilities as a pilot. No 43 Squadron was a fighter unit, flying Armstrong Whitworth Siskin IIIA single-seat aircraft, and was regarded as an élite unit within the RAF at that period. Its commander, when Esmonde joined the squadron, was Squadron Leader C.N. Lowe MC, DFC (later, Group Captain, Retd), a veteran fighter ace of the 1914-18 war who established a huge reputation post-1918 as an English international rugby three-quarter, gaining more caps than any predecessor.

Lowe's dedication and constant enthusiasm for flying, and especially his determination to raise 43 Squadron's already high reputation to the peak of perfection in all things was in part illustrated by the comment of his Adjutant, Flying Officer G.R.A. Elsmie to a newly-arrived pilot, 'Go to the tarmac. The CO is never in his office; he's either in the air or on the tarmac.'

This new arrival, Ian Brodie, then a Flight Lieutenant but ultimately to rise to Air Commodore, OBE, recalled; 'We had ten officers and six Sergeant pilots and fifty-eight NCOs and airmen. We were – happily – self-contained for maintenance. I write happily because the squadron spirit was wonderful. There was no stuffiness as between officers and airmen ... we were a very happy squadron, worked hard and played hard, and the relationship between all ranks was unusually close.'*

In the mode of the period, a fighter squadron's flying skills and disciplines were personified by formation aerobatics, and in the year 1930, when Eugene Esmonde was with the unit, 43 Squadron achieved not only perfection in such aerial routines, but introduced an entirely novel 'improvement' during the eleventh annual RAF Display at Hendon on 28 June. Led by Squadron Leader Lowe, nine of the squadron's Siskins took off in three Vics of three, each Vic having long rubber cords attacked from one Siskin to another. Their subsequent display routine of 'tied-together' aerobatics drew fulsome praise from the aeronautical press. *Flight* magazine (4 July 1930) described their performance as:

> The gem of the whole Display ... this came on at 4.39 pm, and
> the squadron had been splendidly trained, and it was splendidly

*43 Squadron by J. Beedle; Beaumont Aviation Literature, 1966.

Armstrong Whitworth Atlas of No. 26 Squadron RAF.

No. 43 Squadron's aerobatic team, 1930. Rear, L-R: Fg Off R.F. Fletcher, Plt Offs Heber-Percy & R. Elsmie. Front, L-R: Fg Off E.R. Simmonds; Flt Lt I.E. Brodie; Flt Lt E. Thornton; Sqn Ldr C.N. Lowe, MC, DFC (OC Sqn); Flt Lt C.T. 'Panshine' Walkington; Fg Off R. Barrett; Fg Off E. Esmonde. Photo taken in front of a squadron AW Siskin fighter at RAF Tangmere.

Close-up of Eugene Esmonde from previous view.

led by Squadron Leader C.N. Lowe, MC, DFC. The squadron took off in squadron formation and then changed to Flights astern. The 'wheel' as they changed direction at the end of the aerodrome was one of the prettiest manoeuvres of all … In each manoeuvre the squadron showed the most perfect training and accuracy of drill. It was a most finished display.

Even the notoriously blunt-spoken C.G. Grey, editor of *Aeroplane* magazine, was unreserved in his praise, terming 43's efforts, 'The team work and the handling of the machines were quite perfect' – praise indeed! The standard demonstrated at Hendon was to be maintained thereafter. Towards the end of 1930, for example, 43 Squadron repeated its aerobatic routine for the benefit of VIPs attending the Empire Prime Ministers' Conference at Croydon aerodrome. Despite very blustery winds and a broken cloud base of only some 800 feet, the Siskins performed to perfection; though after the second of two successive loops in squadron formation the Siskins came out of their resulting dive just *below* the level of the top of the airfield control tower in which the VIPs were standing – some distinguished heads were seen to duck!

Lest it be thought that Esmonde and his fellow pilots spent all their time indulging in 'pretty flying', it should be noted that in 1930 the squadron achieved second place in the Command Air-to-Ground Firing competition; B Flight won the Chalmers Trophy, and C Flight came a narrow second place in the Sassoon Cup navigation contest. Such achievements emphasised the unit's application to its prime functions of a firstline fighter squadron, in itself yet another tribute to the leadership qualities of Squadron Leader Lowe and the professionalism of his air and ground crews.

In November 1930 Lowe was succeeded in command of 43 Squadron by Squadron Leader Lionel H. Slatter, ODE, DSC, DFC, late of the RAF's High Speed Flight of Schneider Trophy fame. Slatter's arrival coincided with rumours of impending fresh equipment for the squadron to replace its ageing Siskins; 'grapevine chatter' which defied tradition by becoming fact in early 1931 when 43 Squadron was selected to be the first unit to receive a full complement of the sleek, 200 mph Hawker Fury I interceptor-fighter aircraft, and by the end of May 1931 the squadron possessed

AW Siskin IIIAs of 43 Squadron, displaying the unit markings of black & white checks.

sixteen of the new machines.

Eugene Esmonde, however, had no opportunity to test his skills in a Fury, being posted from the squadron on 3 May to RAF Gosport, Hampshire. By then promoted to Flying Officer (seniority from 28 June 1930), Esmonde was now to undergo a 16-week course of instruction in the handling of aircraft operating from aircraft carriers and associated naval-air lore as a preliminary to joining a Fleet Air Arm unit for active duty. The Gosport course concentrated to a large degree on deck-landing techniques and, especially, torpedo-dropping tactics, apart from its general inculcation of 'land-lubber' RAF personnel into the esoteric routines of Royal Navy life afloat and ashore. On completion of the course, Esmonde was duly posted on 25 October 1931 to No 463 Fleet Torpedo Bomber (FTB) Flight of the Fleet Air Arm (FAA).

No 463 (FTB) Flight was one of several FAA Flights embarked on the aircraft carrier *Courageous*, which had been re-commissioned at Portsmouth in September 1930 for service with the Home Fleet. When Esmonde joined it the Flight was equipped with Blackburn Dart torpedo-bombers, an aircraft of ungainly, near-elephantine appearance with a performance range in keeping with its looks – a vast change for Esmonde after a year of flying the agile Siskins of 43 Squadron.

The FAA complement of HMS *Courageous* at that time was under the command of Wing Commander Raymond Collishaw, DSO, OBE, DSC, DFC, the Canadian top-scoring fighter ace of the 1914-18 Royal Naval Air Service, whose command comprised a total of nine FAA Flights, flying variously Fairey IIIFs and Flycatchers and Blackburn Darts, apart from some Avro 504N Lynx trainers.

Esmonde's first take-off, circuit, and landing back on the deck of *Courageous* was watched – like every newly-joined pilot's efforts – critically by the remaining RAF and RN personnel, and was, in their generally expert opinion, the best 'off-and-on' effort any pilot aboard had made to date. Unfortunately for Esmonde, however, this approval was not shared by the Lieutenant-Commander commanding 463 Flight, resulting in some uncomfortable minutes weathering the subsequent storm of abuse from his 'boss'. It was the start of a clash of personalities between Esmonde and his Flight commander which was to be the tenor of Esmonde's remaining

Flight Lieutenant Paull landing a Blackburn Dart of No. 463 FTB Flight, FAA aboard HMAC *Courageous*, 1929.

HM Aircraft Carrier *Courageous*.

service with 463 Flight, despite his popularity with all other members of the unit. Eugene accepted this situation with characteristic stoicism, continued to give of his best, and in his off-duty hours patiently studied towards his goal of an RAF permanent commission.

Though primarily part of the Home Fleet, the *Courageous* in 1931-32 became virtually a 'show-the-flag' ambassador on various occasions. On 12 January 1932, for example, the carrier sailed for Gibraltar to join the annual Spring Cruise, including visits to Malta, Vatika Bay, and Lisbon. The latter venue was reached on 4 March, when the carrier treated the local population to a mini-display of its air strength. To quote the contemporary *Aeroplane* report (9 March 1932):

> Just about 9 am the approach of the *Courageous* was heralded by successive waves of British aeroplanes which flew in perfect formations until they were over Lisbon where they gave a faultless exhibition of changing formation. Other machines then gave a display of aerobatics from such a great height that they could be seen for miles around. Wing-tip flares and smoke trails were used effectively and one part of the exhibition was a kind of circus, in the course of which the larger machines flew in a large circle of smoke, with the smaller fighters looping and generally cavorting in the middle. Altogether it was a very fine display ... what impressed us most was the astonishing accuracy of the station-keeping and the perfection of the aerobatics.

On 8 March the carrier was visited by the President of the Portuguese Republic, and *Courageous* finally returned to Portsmouth on 13 March. Her stay in 'Pompey' was brief, however, and on 26 April she left again for a cruise of Home Waters, visiting Loch Erriboll, Scapa Flow, Larne, Torbay, then returned to Portsmouth on 29 June.

The carrier's return left its personnel with merely two weeks in which to prepare for a royal visit, because on 12 July HM King George V came aboard for his Review of the Fleet which took place off Portland. In order to show the Sovereign how the Fleet Air Arm operated, a special 'grandstand' was constructed abaft the carrier's

Touch-down. A 463 Flight Dart comes aboard HMAC *Courageous*, 1929.

Vickers Virginia – 'Ginny' – of No. 7 Squadron RAF.

funnel, on the level of the flying bridge, from which the King was able to view various take-offs, landings, and aerial salutes.

Once the pomp and ceremony were over, the carrier's company began a more leisurely preparation for yet another cruise in Home Waters. At the same period, late August, command of the FAA aboard *Courageous* was handed over by Wing Commander Collishaw to Esmonde's former commander on 43 Squadron, Wing Commander Lionel Slatter. This next cruise included visiting Rosyth and Banff, then the carrier sailed back to Portsmouth for a refit. On return to 'base' Esmonde left the carrier, being posted back to Gosport on 20 October 1932. His year with the FAA had been one of expanding experience and personal enjoyment, albeit an extremely hard-working period. The one black spot of the year had been his disappointment at failing to obtain a high enough grading in the specialist examination he sat in December 1931 which, had he passed, would have led to his permanent RAF commission.

It is perhaps ironic that at almost any other period of RAF history Eugene Esmonde might have reasonably consoled himself for his examination failure with the thought that, with average luck he might be permitted to re-sit an equivalent examination within a year's time or so. However, 1931-32 were crucial years for the RAF in the context of severe economic cutbacks in financial support, due primarily to a deep world depression in general and home-grown political exigencies. The RAF's budget for 1931-32 amounted to a net total of £18,100,000 only, and the Service suffered a number of curbs and restrictions affecting virtually all facets of equipment, personnel and recruitment, and including an across-the-board pay reduction for all ranks; all part of the governmental scheme of National Economy. The effect of all these strictures was a Service with relatively few vacancies to fill, and more applicants to fill such vacancies than the RAF could ever accept. Thus, selection of candidates for long-term service i.e. permanent commissions mainly favoured the RAF's own products – ex-Cranwell and Halton men – before spreading the net to other forms of Service entry personnel.

For Esmonde, in late 1932, there was the worrying prospect of merely one more year on the RAF's active list, then virtual discharge into civilian life at a time of mass unemployment. Convinced by then that flying was the best career for him, he set out to accumulate as much air experience as possible in the time left to him, and preferably in a variety of aircraft types to broaden his knowledge. From November 1932 he was employed as an instructor at Gosport, teaching naval-air techniques to RAF and FAA tyro crews about to undertake tours of duty at sea. One of his pupils remembers Esmonde as, 'A quietly spoken man, looking somewhat older than his real age. He knew precisely what he needed from me in terms of flying and was equally precise in his teaching technique. He never once lost his patience with me, despite several howling errors on my part, but simply explained in detail what I'd done wrong, then proceeded to demonstrate the correct method or procedure. This approach – such a contrast to some short-tempered instructors I'd met in my original flying tuition – gave me the necessary confidence to complete the course without any major upsets.'

On 10 April 1933 Esmonde left Gosport and reported to his next unit, No 7 Squadron at Worthy Down, Hampshire. Commanded by Wing Commander (later Group Captain) A.L. Gregory, MBE, MC, No 7 Squadron was a heavy (*sic*) bomber unit, flying somewhat ancient Vickers Virginias. The lumbering 'Ginnies', as these aircraft were usually dubbed, if near-obsolete by 1933, at least provided Eugene with further experience in handling a multi-engined large aircraft, both by day and by night. For the following eight months Esmonde seized every available opportunity to pile up flying hours, participating in various air exercises and pseudo night-bombing flights; then, on 28 December 1933, he was officially transferred to the Class 'A' Reserve. His total time in the RAF had seen him accumulate 855 flying hours, in addition to which he had qualified himself for a 2nd Class Navigator's Certificate. Though to all intents a civilian again, he remained in the RAF Reserve for four years, being duly promoted to Flight Lieutenant with effect from 1 April 1936.

CHAPTER FOUR

Fresh Horizons

Eugene Esmonde's release from the active list of the Royal Air Force in December 1933 came as something of a double regret for him. His varied experiences with the RAF and the Fleet Air Arm had been almost wholly pleasurable and stimulating, and he had clearly enjoyed the comradeship and close community atmosphere of RAF service life and routine; indeed, one contemporary opined that his RAF years had been ' ... the peak of Eugene's life'. Equally, his love for flying had been firmly entrenched, leaving him with a conviction that in aviation lay his future.

Objectively viewed, his qualifications and prospects for any such career in civil aviation were at that time fairly slim. His total flying time was less than the 1,000 hours minimum usually required of potential civil airline pilots; moreover, much of his RAF piloting had been in aircraft types, e.g. fighters and trainers, which offered no direct application to civil flying beyond demonstrating his natural skills and adaptability. As to actual employment as a civilian pilot, there were in the early 1930s any number of private flying clubs and associations into which Esmonde might well have been welcomed as a 'staff' pilot and/or instructor. However, none of these could truly guarantee any form of long-term career or security; something Esmonde particularly required of any future appointment. Accordingly, he next considered the various private airlines then operating from Britain, both internal and trans-Europe. Again, most of these (if not all) appeared to offer little more than short-term engagements, with small prospects of eventual permanence of employment. There seemed to be only one possibility left to him, assuming he wished to remain mainly based in the United Kingdom; the sole national airline of the era, Imperial Airways Ltd.

As the 'chosen instrument' of the British government's

contemporary Imperial Policy to develop British commercial air transportation on a sound economic basis, Imperial Airways Ltd had come into being legally on 31 March 1924, having amalgamated the existing air fleets of four pioneering civil airlines i.e. Handley Page Ltd, Instone Air Line Ltd, Daimler Airway, and British Marine Air Navigation Ltd. As with all facets of British civil aviation, the new company came under the aegis of the Department of Civil Aviation, an integral part of the Air Ministry, which department had been originally created on 12 February 1919.

The main difference between the status of Imperial Airways and all other civil airlines, however, was that while still ostensibly a private company – it initially floated a capital of one million pounds – only Imperial Airways received governmental backing from its outset with a subsidy of a further million pounds, albeit spread over a ten year period. Thus this curious combination of a public company *and* a government undertaking, while providing a public service, was also a virtual monopoly of official priorities in such matters as financial support, licensing of fresh aerial routes, *et al.*

During its first ten years' existence Imperial Airways grew from its initial fleet of seventeen aircraft (of eight different designs) to nearly forty machines, and slowly but steadily extended its scheduled aerial services and routes around Europe, at the same time cautiously beginning to survey and explore fresh routes eastwards and southwards, reaching out to the furthest countries and territories of the vast global British Empire of the 1920-30s. By 1928, in which year the new London Airport at Croydon came into full operation, Imperial Airways in close conjunction with the overseas-based RAF had already opened or proved air routes from Britain to most parts of the Middle East, Africa, India, and Australia. These pioneering projects were approved by the British government to the extent that on 1 April 1929 a new ten-year agreement between the Air Ministry and Imperial Airways came into effect, with agreed subsidies for European and England-to-India routes amounting overall to almost two and a half million pounds on a gently diminishing scale annually. Such a gesture of confidence in the company's future – the original ten-years' agreement had been intended to be the only such subsidy contract – meant that the foreseeable future of Imperial Airways appeared secure; an investment understandably welcomed by the company's air and ground staffs.

Thus, by 1934, when Eugene Esmonde was casting around for acceptable employment as a pilot, the company seemed his best option and he duly applied and was accepted into the company's service as a First Officer; an appointment equivalent to Second or Co-pilot who, though a qualified pilot, 'assisted' the principal pilot, or Captain, in his duties, occasionally taking over control of an aircraft to 'spell' the Captain on lengthy flights.

Though reasonably well qualified to take the controls of most existing aircraft in use, and with the advantage of his Second Class Navigator's Certificate, Esmonde's flying record at the moment of joining Imperial Airways rather paled in comparison with some of the much more senior and experienced skippers of the company. Men like the piratically-bearded O.P. Jones, F.J. Bailey, F. Dudley Travers, W. Armstrong, L.A. Walters, H.H. Perry, the South African R.F. Caspareuthus, E.S. Alcock, A.S. Wilcockson, and others; virtually all pilots who had flown on operations with the Royal Flying Corps or Royal Naval Air Service during the 1914-18 war, and then turned their skills and courage to pioneering the peacetime embryo civil air lines in Britain. By 1934 the whole business of air line transportation in the European context had become not so much pioneering as near-routine. Scheduled services were maintained almost to the advertised minute, regular and increasingly accepted by the lay public as a normal form of transport. Air liners on the regular runs offered comparative luxury to passengers, including four-course dinners, luncheons, and teas of first-rate quality, steward-served, and at quite reasonable prices. Moreover, the safety record of Imperial Airways was second to none, with only an occasional unavoidable accident to aircraft but no passenger casualties. The greatest 'enemy' remained weather conditions, particularly dense fog or excessively high winds.

Even these problems were slowly being overcome, with new yet simple radio aids, though sheer skill on the part of aircraft captains was often the criterion. It was not unknown in thick fog conditions, for example, for a white chalk line to be drawn on the surface of Croydon's airfield in the desired take-off direction, then have an aircraft taxy slowly out in the wake of a tractor to the 'start line' of

Armstrong Whitworth Argosy, G-AACH, *'City of Edinburgh'*.

Short Scylla, G-ACJJ, which was eventually wrecked in a gale at Drem, April 1940.

Handley Page HP42, G-AAXE, *'Hengist'*.
Armstrong Whitworth Atlanta, *'Aurora'* during WW2 this aircraft served with No. 31 Squadron RAF in India and Iraq.

the chalk. Once there, and ensuring that as the aircraft gathered speed it maintained its direction vis-à-vis the chalk line, yet another scheduled take-off was accomplished.

If the European operations of Imperial Airways had achieved such normality by 1934, the same could not be said wholly of the company's ventures in the far eastern extensions of its services. In India, Malaya, Burma, etc there was still much to be accomplished, despite the trojan work already undertaken in previous years. It might well be said to be an area of potential still very much of a pioneering nature. It was to this area of operations that Eugene Esmonde was posted after his induction in 1934, a stint of overseas duty which was to last for some two years. His initial posting was to the headquarters of No 2 Operating Division, Imperial Airways at Karachi, India, arriving there early in 1935. His arrival coincided with an important stage of progress by Imperial Airways towards a long-sought aerial route from England to Australia staging across India. The trans-India stages of such a proposed route had been a bone of contention between Britain, India, and Australia since 1920, hampered continually by financial crises and, no less, by Indian nationalism. After many years of unfruitful negotiations and proposals by all parties concerned, however, in mid-1933 a hybrid company, Indian Trans-Continental Airways, was created – hybrid in the context that Imperial Airways owned 51 per cent of the company stock, and the Indian government the remaining 49 per cent.

The company was created primarily to operate the route from Karachi to Rangoon, and eventually to Singapore, for which purpose Karachi was the 'base' for four Armstrong Whitworth XV four-engined monoplane aircraft; *Aurora* (G-ABTM) and *Arethusa* (G-ABPI), registered respectively VT-AEG and VT-AEF with the India Trans-Continental Airways, and *Astraea* and *Athena*, still registered G-ABTL and G-ABTK with Imperial Airways. Later these were to be joined by AW XVs *Artemis* (G-ABTJ) and the second-named *Atlanta* (G-ABTI).

At Karachi Esmonde initially became First Officer to Captain Roland Alderson, on whom he left a lasting impression: 'When he [Esmonde] came out to Karachi he soon showed he was the best First Officer to be sent to us there. He was a very competent pilot –

and W/T operator, as was necessary in our two-man crew of the *Atlanta*-class aircraft, and his early promotion to Captain was a foregone conclusion. He was unassuming but a great personality, and had a sense of humour which was inexhaustible.'

Alderson's comment on Eugene's competence as a pilot is significant, in that until joining Imperial Airways Esmonde's only real experience flying multi-engined aircraft had been in the ancient Virginia bombers of No 7 Squadron RAF during his final months of RAF service. Nevertheless, during his first year with Imperial Airways prior to moving to India, Esmonde had accumulated many hours as First Officer on tri-engined Armstrong Whitworth *Argosy*, and four-engined Short *Scylla* and Handley Page 42 air liners; all part of the normal introductory training with Imperial Airways, but accentuated by Esmonde's characteristic determination to learn everything possible about his profession and to broaden his experience. His constant wish to fly added more hours during 1935 and early 1936, completing numerous trips around India and south to Singapore, and by mid-1936 Esmonde received his promotion to Captain, still flying AW XV aircraft from the Karachi base airfield. By then his popularity with the other Imperial Airways staff was widespread, and not merely amongst his fellow air crews but including the ground maintenance crews.

David Humphries was an engineer with Imperial Airways based at Karachi during Esmonde's service there; 'I first met Esmonde in Karachi when he was flying Armstrong Whitworth *Atlanta*-class aircraft between Karachi and Singapore, with a 48-hours' stopover at each end of the route. The pilots would frequently drop into our Mess for a drink before going off to their hotels, and one night we invited him to our monthly guest-night dinner. He came and, after dinner, gave an impromptu talk on his experiences flying the Empire routes and in the Fleet Air Arm. He was only twenty-six years old then but was widely travelled, with a good mind and a terrific Irish sense of fun. Even through a slightly alcoholic haze I remember being deeply impressed with his breadth of knowledge and his sense of humour. After this the evening degenerated into a typical Mess night with a game called "Are you there, Moriarty?", a six-a-side rugger on the lawn, in both of which he participated and indeed initiated wholeheartedly. He was in appearance rather

De Havilland 86 (L) and AW Atlanta, VT-AEG at Dum Dum airport, Calcutta, India, 1936.

The airship shed hangar at Drigh Road, Karachi, India, 1936.

Hangar scene at Drigh Road, Karachi, with AW Atlanta *Astraea*.

Imperial Airways (later, BOAC) flying boat terminal at Hythe, Hampshire, showing the main mooring jetty and one of the floating jetties (left).

short, with dark hair and a boyish face, normally thoughtful which would break into a wonderful smile when he was amused.

'As I've said, he had a marvellous Irish sense of humour, but also a complete and utter dedication to his job, and was a superb pilot. I was a passenger on one of his flights between Karachi and Singapore and we were flying along the Burmese coast in tropical monsoon rain. Anyone who's had experience of monsoon weather will know what it was like, with rain coming down in a solid sheet, and Esmonde was fighting the controls every inch of the way. The visibility was so bad that the only way he could see where he was going was by following the coast line at almost sea level. When we reached Akyab the aerodrome looked like, and almost was, a lake, and our landing must have looked like a flying boat landing. It was a superb feat of airmanship. My admiration for him, both as a man and as a pilot, was profound, and I was not surprised when I heard he won a VC – it was typical of the man.'

In mid-1936 Esmonde was detached to the Irrawaddy Flotilla Company in Burma, being based at Rangoon, where he piloted the company's two Short Scion Senior four-engined floatplanes, VT-AGU and VT-AHI, on internal feeder line flights. Even this fairly mundane occupation was not without risk, and on one occasion his aircraft suddenly stalled and fell headlong into the Irrawaddy river; luckily without injury to Esmonde. Then, in early 1937, he was succeeded in this appointment by John Main-Waddell, later Lieutenant-Commander, RNVR(A), an old acquaintance from his Fleet Air Arm days, and eventually returned to England to be based at Hythe in Hampshire. At Hythe Esmonde immediately commenced conversion under supervision for eventual command of the Short S.23 Empire-class flying boats then in service with Imperial Airways, being supervised by Captain R.F. Caspareuthus, a South African veteran skipper who, forty years later, still remembered Eugene as 'Extremely popular with all pilots, and a truly lovely character.'

Nor was that popularity confined to fellow pilots; one of the female administrative staff, Miss E.V. Stone, remembering Eugene Esmonde as, ' ... this quiet, courteous man, always a favourite in the typists' room, where we voted him "one of the best".'

It took little time before Esmonde qualified for command of a

Short Empire flying boat, but all his skills were needed on his first trip as Captain. Flying home to Hythe from Alexandria, Egypt, via Athens, Brindisi, and Rome, he landed outside the harbour at Marignane, Marseilles during a fierce mistral and on heavy seas. The control launch attempted valiantly to reach the flying boat but failed to make contact, leaving Esmonde in a highly vulnerable situation, fraught with dangers. Coolly, Esmonde manoeuvred the aircraft into the main teeth of the high winds so that it began to be literally blown backwards, then by judicious use of its engines, he began guiding the aircraft through the narrow harbour entrance. To accomplish this highly delicate manoeuvre it was necessary for his First Officer to take up a position on the top of the hull, clinging for dear life and able to shout steering instructions to Esmonde, who, naturally, was completely unsighted rearwards of his aircraft. With little margin for error, the 'backing-up' movement into the relative safety of the small harbour was finally accomplished – a feat of sheer skill later acclaimed by the local manager, ground staff and passengers alike as 'brilliant'.

Quite apart from the pure technical skills displayed during this incident, Esmonde had also unconsciously demonstrated a particular trait in his character, that of always placing his full confidence and faith in the abilities of his crew members. Throughout his years of command with both Imperial Airways and, later, the Fleet Air Arm, Esmonde never failed to exercise his authority as commander, accepting ultimate responsibility for his crew or unit's activities at all times, but equally with complete faith in his fellow men to whom he invariably gave effective clear orders, without fuss or follow-up, expecting them to know and do whatever was necessary without interference. Without any apparently conscious effort, Esmonde as a commander always maintained an exact balance between the authority and dignity of his position and his unfailing friendliness towards all men; a gift of nature relatively rare amongst those appointed in command of others. Such trust gave his subordinates not only respect for their superior officer, but increased confidence in themselves. Undoubtedly Esmonde's respect for his fellow men derived from his deep Catholic faith, as indeed did his inherited code of loyalty and honour.

Imperial Airways' new flying boat base at Hythe had been

Eugene Esmonde (left) relaxing at the Singapore Swimming club, September 1937.

Short S.23 Empire-class flying boat, 'Cavalier' of Imperial airways (G-ADUU).

opened officially on 5 March 1937 – from which date Empire air services by landplanes from Croydon ceased, being (until the outbreak of war in 1939) solely the base for European services thereafter – which arrangement left Esmonde and the other flying boat skippers and crews the routine but pleasant near-monopoly of flights to Middle and Far Eastern venues. By the beginning of 1938 no less than twenty-two of the graceful Short 'Empire' flying boats had been delivered to Imperial Airways for those overseas routes, though three of these – *Capricornus* (G-ADVA), *Courtier* (G-ADVC), and *Cygnus* (G-ADUZ) – had been lost in crashes, involving five passenger deaths and many others injured, before the end of 1937. By late 1938 an improved variant of the design, the design, the Short S.30, was about to enter airline service, specifically for trans-Atlantic flights to Bermuda, while other S.30s introduced in December 1938 incorporated greatly increased fuel tankage and inflight-refuelling apparatus to permit greater range and endurance performances. Esmonde, however, remained principally employed on the well-established staging routes from Hythe to India and Singapore, and, like all other experienced Captains, spent many of such flights inculcating newly-joined First Officers into the arts of handling the 'Empire' flying boats in the widely varying climates and conditions to be met en route.

One of the many First Officers to be nurtured by Eugene Esmonde at that time was an Australian, Oscar Garden, previously employed as a pilot with Imperial Airways' rival independent airline, British Airways.* Garden transferred to Imperial Airways in late 1938 in order to undertake conversion training in flying boats, with the eventual aim of joining Tasman Airways in his native country when this became officially constituted. Garden's recollection of his initiation period with Imperial Airways is not without interest in reflecting the era.

'I had quite a few trips as First Officer with a number of Imperial Airways' captains and it was quite a shattering experience at times, coming from British Airways' intensive pilot training to what seemed pretty haphazard training in Imperial Airways! However,

---

* British Airways, initially formed in late 1935, eventually was merged with Imperial Airways in 1939 to form British Overseas Airways Corporation (BOAC).

there was one bright spot amongst all the variety, and that was the wonderful experience of having Eugene Esmonde as flight Captain. Unlike a number of the other pilots with whom I flew, he gave me all the assistance one could expect to help my conversion to marine aircraft, and it was, as you might say, a pleasure to do business with him. In fact, I was very lucky to strike him on my very first co-pilot trip. It left Hythe on 14 December 1938 and arrived at Karachi on 18 December, leaving Karachi the same day and eventually arriving back in England on 31 December. The delay in getting home again was caused by extremely bad weather and we were stuck, with several other flying boat crews, at Marseilles. In the end we were all flown back to Croydon in a dreadful aircraft called *Albatross*, a De Havilland so-called airliner, and frankly I was thankful to get out of it, as was Esmonde!*

'I will always remember Esmonde for two things apart from his unselfish help with my conversion training. At Karachi Esmonde arrived at the Imperial Airways' pilots' Mess and made straight for the bar, where the barman placed a bottle of Drambuie with a glass in front of him and then left him to it. Esmonde imbibed the Drambuie until he'd had a little more than enough, then went to bed with some assistance from me. Apparently this ritual was a regular thing and he was first class company. The second thing I remember clearly was his describing Juba, a refuelling stop in southern Sudan, as "every take-off from there is a potential accident" – he was dead right on that score too …'.

Another First Officer to receive part of his 'tutelage' from Eugene Esmonde was the late Captain H.L.M. Glover, who said of him; 'I first met him early in 1938 at Hythe. He was then a Captain and I did trips as his First Officer to Kisumu, Kenya and to Singapore. I found him a lively, interesting and charming man, always full of fun and humour. Our voyages were not without incident. For example, on 13 March 1939 in the flying boat *RMA Coolangatta* (VH-ABB), we were unable to alight at Bahrein because of dense fog, so Esmonde put her down on the sea a few miles out. The passengers were then served with breakfast and when the fog started rolling

* De Havilland DH91 Albatross '*Frobisher*' (G-AFDI) which had been returning from an experimental Christmas mail run to Cairo, Egypt.

Eugene Esmonde (right) with Ronald Ballantine (left) and friend enjoy a snack between races at Bukit Timah Racecourse, Singapore, 1936.

Short Empire-class flying boat VH-ABB, *'Coolangatta'*, flown by Esmonde on occasion. Eventually wrecked in Sydney Harbour on 11 October 1944 when serving with QANTAS.

towards us he calmly took off and alighted further away. All quite unofficial, of course!'

This last incident occurred at a time when Eugene Esmonde was reconsidering his continuance in the employ of Imperial Airways. Legally, he was still a Flight Lieutenant in the RAF Reserve, Class 'A', and in the wake of the Munich Crisis of September 1938 he, like most thinking men, felt that war with Hitler's Nazi Germany was still a distinct possibility within a year or so. Technically, as an Irish-born subject, he might well remain neutral in the event of any Anglo-Nazi conflict, but such a thought did not appeal to Esmonde. Then, in January 1939, he received a letter from the Admiralty, offering him a commission in the Royal Navy's Fleet Air Arm' ... in a position of responsibility'.

The offer was sufficiently vague as to rank and appointment to make Esmonde hesitate to accept. His contemporary position with Imperial Airways was well paid, his seniority and experience as a Captain augured well for future appointments to higher executive responsibilities; indeed, a secure future in civil aviation. He then received a further offer from the Admiralty, including specifically a commission in the Fleet Air Arm as a Lieutenant-Commander(A), with a guarantee of fifteen years' regular service, and the probability of further regular engagement thereafter.

Having celebrated his thirtieth birthday on 1 March, Eugene Esmonde recognised that such a definite offer had many advantages for him and therefore, being privately delighted at the prospect of a return to the esoteric community atmosphere of Service life, he duly accepted this latest Admiralty offer. Accordingly, he was officially discharged from his RAF Reserve commitment, and was enlisted as a Lieutenant-Commander(A) in the Fleet Air Arm with effect from 14 April 1939, with seniority in his rank dating from 1 January 1939. By then Esmonde had accumulated an overall total of 5,500 flying hours during his years with the RAF and Imperial Airways, apart from relatively vast experience on a global basis in both land and marine aircraft of many differing types.

Captain Eugene Esmonde in his Imperial Airways uniform.

CHAPTER FIVE

Sea Wings

When Eugene Esmonde transferred to active duty with the Royal Navy's Air Branch in April 1939, he became a member of a relatively small but hastily expanding air arm which, while retaining the title of Fleet Air Arm, had only begun to come under the total control of the Admiralty less than two years before, when on 30 July 1937 the Prime Minister, Neville Chamberlain, had announced that decision. Since the 'forced marriage' on 1 April 1918 of the FAA's parent Royal Naval Air Service with the Army's Royal Flying Corps to give birth to the Royal Air Force, control of maritime aviation Services had been the focal point of protracted and bitterly contested debates within Britain's armed Services and the political corridors of power. The lengthy inter-Service controversy, spiced with prejudice, ignorance, and die-hard attitudes, had left the tiny Fleet Air Arm as an illegitimate child as far as the Lordships of the Admiralty were concerned, while its legal master, the RAF, tended to regard the FAA as something of a poor relation in the context of provision of updated aircraft specifically designed for the peculiar FAA air-sea role.

Actual administrative control of the Fleet Air Arm was not assumed by the Admiralty until 24 May 1939, on which date the Admiralty took over four former RAF stations and retitled these, in RN tradition, as 'ships' i.e. Lee-on-Solent (HMS *Daedalus*), Ford (HMS *Peregrine*), Worthy Down (HMS *Kestrel*), and Donibristle (HMS *Merlin*). On that same date the hitherto curious system of 'dual commissions' – RAF 'shadow ranks' held by RN officers serving with the FAA – also ceased; whilst an RN Flag Officer, Rear Admiral Richard Bell Davies, VC, DSO, AFC, was appointed Rear Admiral, Naval Air Stations, based at Lee-on-Solent.

The steady, though tardy, build-up of strength in aircraft and personnel for the Fleet Air Arm, particularly in 1938-39, included no small number of ex-RAF and civil airline pilots. When Eugene Esmonde first donned RN uniform, he was one of six ex-RAF Reserve officers who had very recently transferred to the Fleet Air Arm, one of these being Squadron Leader G.N.P. Stringer DFC, whom Esmonde was to befriend and serve alongside during his first year with the FAA, and was to meet again aboard HMS *Ark Royal* in 1941 when Patrick Stringer was serving as that aircraft carrier's Flight Deck Officer.

Esmonde's first official FAA appointment was to HMS *Victory* ('additional') for full flying duties at the Lee-on-Solent naval air station, where he initially underwent a course of 'refresher' instruction on Walrus amphibian aircraft and aircraft catapulting technique, lasting from 14 April to 30 April 1939, followed by a further week's instruction and practice in Naval Observer duties.

On completion of these training courses he was appointed on 8 May as commander of No 754 Squadron, FAA, still at Lee-on-Solent. His new unit was one of two FAA training squadrons forming No 2 Observers' School, under the charge of Commander W.W.R. Bentinck (later, Captain, OBE, RN, Retd) who was also to meet Esmonde again in 1941 on HMS *Ark Royal* when Bentinck was Commander (Operations) aboard the carrier. The squadron commanded by Esmonde flew Walrus amphibians and Fairey Seafox floatplanes; while its brother unit, No 753 Squadron was commanded by Lieutenant-Commander Patrick Stringer, and flew Blackburn Sharks.

Stringer's recollection of Esmonde during 1939-40 *et al* was as: ' ... a little fellow, smaller than his brother Witham (whom I was to meet at a later date), so when Eugene and I walked to the local club in Lee for a drink, he insisted that I walked in the gutter – I was six feet four inches tall! He was a very devout Catholic and unmarried, saying that he did not think it right to get married while the war was on – that it wasn't fair. He was remarkable to me for his tremendous loyalty to his friends. He would not hear anything against one, and gave one quite undeserved praise.'

It should be added here that while at Lee-on-Solent Esmonde's devotion to his faith led him to take great pains in helping other Roman Catholics on the station, including the provision of regular Service transport for their attendance at Sunday Mass; there being

Esmonde in Lieutenant-Commander, RN uniform outside *Drominagh*, 1939. Note lack of pilot's badge on sleeve as yet.

no appointed RC Chaplain to the FAA at that period.

Esmonde's period of command of No 754 Squadron was to last from 8 May 1939 until 30 May 1940, during which time his crews flew a variety of naval aircraft types, including the Walrus, Sea-fox, one or two Blackburn Rocs, Percival Proctors, and some Fairey Swordfish torpedo-bombers (land and float variants). Each training course lasted twenty-two weeks, comprising some fifty RNVR midshipmen and Sub-Lieutenants(A), and covered such subjects as wireless telegraphy (W/T), navigation, and signals, split fairly evenly between ground classroom theory and aerial practice; all aiming to produce suitably qualified Naval Observers for the FAA's firstline operational units. Also based at Lee-on-Solent was a seaplane training squadron, tasked with 'converting' pilots to floatplanes – such men having first been given their *ab initio* pilot instruction under the auspices of the RAF. Only on completion of their seaplane conversion training could commissioned officers be awarded their flying badges, and rating pilots be promoted to Petty Officer.

While such a training duty was obviously of high importance for the Fleet Air Arm during the first year of the war – the urgent need for increasing numbers of trained air crews escalating rapidly to fill the newly established squadrons and other firstline units – Esmonde began agitating for a more active appointment, stating preference for command of an operational squadron. His request, though sincere, was no bid for excitement or pseudo-glory of frontline combat; simply a perfectly natural desire – shared by many of his contemporaries – to fulfil his ultimate professional *raison d'être* as a member of a fighting Service, sworn to defend and protect a King and country by personal oath of loyalty. If such a desire was (is) considered bordering on pomposity by some, it had no such basis in Eugene Esmonde's character. The inheritor of many centuries of Irish-Norman Catholic blood-lines with their indivisible codes of duty and personal honour, Esmonde's attitudes to the war were strictly professional, devoid of personal hate for the enemy; as witnessed in a brief letter he wrote to his mother from Lee-on-Solent on 20 September 1939, in which he remarked on the loss of the aircraft carrier HMS *Courageous*, sunk by the German submarine *U-29* on 17 September while (ironically) engaged on an

Lieutenant-Commander, RN (left) at Hythe, 1939.

Personnel of No. 754 Sqn, FAA at Lee-on-Solent, 1939. Seated, L-R: Unknown SNCO; Plt Off Fortnum; Plt Off Cutts; Lt Herrior-Hill, RN; Lt-Cdr E. Esmonde, RN (OC Sqn); Lt Newman, RN; Plt Off A. Forbes; Sub-Lt Fox, RN; Unknown CPO, RN.

anti-submarine patrol. For Esmonde this had been something of a personal loss too, because of his RAF service aboard the carrier in 1931-32, saying:

> Poor old *Courageous* has gone! We in the Fleet Air Arm have lost some brave friends but the accounts which we have from our friends, also, who survived this straightforward act of war have been full of heroic details. I have stood upon the bridge of *Courageous* so often that I know every inch, and the reports of the Captain* upon that bridge during the last moments of *Courageous* confirm that the poor old ship had a commander of whom the Royal Navy can be truly proud! Another straightforward act of war and I don't blame either party. Both sides were obeying orders and the individuals are equally fine. For my part I am satisfied that we are on the Christian side.

Esmonde's deep-rooted belief in Britain's 'cause' as a Christian crusade against the evils of Nazism was further reflected in another, later letter to his mother, in which he said in part;

> ... for Heaven's sake if *I* am ever missing I hope it won't upset anyone, because I can think of no greater honour nor a better way of passing into eternity than in the cause for which the Allies are fighting this war. I have painted a Crusader's head on the fin of my aeroplane & it will stay with me to the end.

Lest this apparent religious zeal be regarded as any form of obsession, it should be remarked that while Eugene Esmonde's faith was unwavering, at no time was he ever known to attempt to impose his beliefs on others. One constant facet of Esmonde's outlook on the human race was his deeply-held faith in an essential goodness to be found in all men, provided one looked for it; hence his unbiased attitude to his friends and acquaintances.

Esmonde's request for an operational post was eventually granted on 31 May 1940 with an appointment to the command of

---

* Captain W.T. Makeig-Jones, who remained on his bridge, saluting the flag, as *Courageous* sank.

No 825 Squadron, FAA, a unit with an already long record of firstline action. Originally formed on 8 October 1934 aboard HMS *Eagle* by the retitling of No 824 Squadron, 825 became the first FAA squadron to be fully equipped with Fairey Swordfish torpedo-bombers in mid-1936, and saw virtually continuous service overseas in the Mediterranean and the Indian ocean areas from its birth until the outbreak of war in September 1939, at which time the squadron was disembarked at Dekheila but embarked on HMS *Glorious* in the following month for operations in the Indian ocean on protection of trade shipping routes, working out from Aden.

In January 1940 the *Glorious* refitted at Malta, then sailed to Alexandria, Egypt where 825 Squadron was disembarked for a month. In April 1940, however, the beginning of the Norwegian campaign resulted in *Glorious* being immediately ordered back to England, arriving on 18 April, on which date 825 Squadron was disembarked and became based at HMS *Kestrel* (Worthy Down). In doing so the squadron escaped the fate of other air units aboard *Glorious* when, on 8 June, the carrier was sunk by gunfire from the German battleship *Scharnhorst* with the loss of 1515 lives. On 20 May No 825 Squadron moved based to RAF Detling, Kent for operations under the aegis of RAF Coastal Command, mainly over the English Channel and coastal areas of France.

Arriving at Worthy Down prior to his actual appointment date, Esmonde completed the hand-over formalities of command of No 825 Squadron with his predecessor, Lieutenant-Commander J. Buckley, then moved his unit to Detling and almost immediately commenced operations. These were in the main *ad hoc* sorties on a daily basis, dependent on the latest priorities as the desperate situation in France so quickly deteriorated for the Allied armies there facing the German *blitzkrieg* invasion of the Low Countries and French soil. Normal roles such as anti-submarine patrols, day and night air reconnaissance, and occasional attacks against German E-boats were flown at first, but by the end of May and in the first weeks of June 1940 825's Swordfish were being employed on daylight bombing sorties against German gun batteries, tanks, and transport in the Calais area, and spotting for a bombardment of Calais by the guns of HMS *Arethusa*. These types of operations, perhaps inevitably due to the low performance range of a

Fairey Seafox.

No. 825 Sqn, FAA at Freetown on return from Takoradi, March 1941. Rear: PO Parker; L/A Howes; L/A Russell; L/A Pimlott; L/A Mulloy. Centre: Sub-Lts Meadway; Griffiths; Lawson; Berrill; Lt McLean; Sub-Lts Fraser; Jackson; Hodgetts; Taylor. Seated: Lt G.J Cardew; Lt-Cdr E. Esmonde (OC); Lt Pollard. Aboard HMAC *Furious*.

Swordfish, cost the squadron dear, with an overall loss of eight aircraft.

On 3 July 1940, accordingly, No 825 Squadron was withdrawn from operations for replenishment and refurbishment of its crews and aircraft. Its six weeks of intense operational activities had exhausted and severely tested the squadron's surviving crews, but within the following seven weeks the squadron had worked up to full fighting strength again, and on 5 September was embarked aboard *Furious* for further operations.

The nine Swordfish of 825 Squadron – its full contemporary strength – complemented nine more Swordfish of No 816 Squadron, and nine Blackburn Skua 'fighter-bombers' of No 801 Squadron to make up the *Furious*'s air striking force in September 1940. The carrier then sailed to join the Allied operations against German shipping and shore objectives in Norway. One of the first such sorties flown by Esmonde took place in the early hours of 22 September; a scheduled two Swordfish squadrons' night torpedo attack on enemy shipping at Trondheim, Norway, to be led by Esmonde.

His Telegraphist Air Gunner (TAG) in Swordfish 'K' was Petty Officer Parker, while his Observer was Lieutenant J.G. Cardew. The latter had joined 825 Squadron in August 1940, with some four years' flying experience in his log book, including much practical knowledge and experience in the relatively new Air to Surface Vessel (ASV) radar airborne aid. Cardew's notes of this, his first sortie with Esmonde, are of particular interest in highlighting the various difficulties met by the Swordfish crews that night:

> Esmonde was leading the two Swordfish squadrons of nine aircraft each. The plan was to cross the coast some fifty miles north of the entrance of the fiord leading to Trondheim, drop right down on to the water of the fiord leading north-east from Trondheim, and attack on a south-westerly course. The moon would be silhouetting the target area. On reaching the coast we found the cloud base was down to below 1,000 feet. The maps we had were atrocious, out of date, and inaccurate. There was no way we could reach the inner fiord as a co-ordinated strike force even if we could manage to miss the mountains.

It would mean blind flying, blind navigation, and a blind let-down into the fiord where we had no knowledge of the cloud base height. We could not fly in through Trondheim fiord as this was heavily protected with guns and wires stretching across the fiord. Both ways in would be suicidal. Esmonde wanted to press on over the mountains. We had a flaming row in the aircraft for about five minutes. I could not pull rank on him but had to convince him through experience that should he press on with the attack eighteen very valuable aircraft and crews would certainly be lost. Our secondary target, namely to seek and destroy enemy coastal shipping, had been given to us in case we should encounter exactly these conditions. Seventeen aircraft were following us in sub-Flights as we circled a couple of miles off the coast whilst Esmonde and I had the argument – eventually common sense (I think) won and I passed the order by light to break formation and to seek and attack shipping.

After about 15 minutes we spotted a German sloop or escort vessel at anchor close under the cliffs. We circled to identify it as German. On the run in we were challenged but no guns opened fire. At about 300 yards Esmonde dropped the torpedo. It was perfectly sighted but it failed to go off. Maybe the depth setting was too great, although as far as I remember we were using the new magnetic type pistol. At least three crews of 825 Squadron failed to return to *Furious*, mainly I fear through Observer error. *Furious* had been at sea for about four days in baddish weather, therefore our take-off position could have been a few miles in error. Possibly the young Observers took their return departure from a known position on the coast and so failed to find the carrier, whereas the experienced Observers noted the error from the landfall position and corrected accordingly.

Esmonde's initial intention, despite all odds against it, of pressing on to the primary target here – a decision which led to him gaining a somewhat unpopular reputation among the 825 Squadron crews as 'bull-headed' and a commander who never considered pros and cons of any operation but simply attacked a target heedlessly – might be explained by his relative inexperience of actual naval air warfare at that time. No one questioned his obvious experience and

Fairey Swordfish of 825 Squadron gets airborne from HMAC *Furious*.

skill as a pure pilot, but operational flying called for more than pure pilotage skill, especially in a leader of any such sortie, where success – and human lives – depended upon a commander's decisions when unexpected situations cropped up which had not been foreseen in the pre-flight briefing. Only the hard school of sheer experience could produce a 'rounded' leader who could adapt immediately to each circumstance encountered. Esmonde had yet to reach that stage of operational maturity. To him, orders were orders, to be carried out at all costs; a conviction he was never to alter, although as his operational experience increased later he was able to temper such rigidity of interpretation of orders with cool reasoning.

Three days after the Trondheim operation Esmonde flew from the *Furious* to the naval air station at Hatston, then next day to Evanton, in order to start collecting replacement aircraft and crews to bring his squadron up to strength again; then instituted a concentrated programme of training for his crews to attain full efficiency once more, finally returning to *Furious* as a complete unit on (or about) 10 October. Just six days later 825 Squadron took part in a bombing strike against Tromso, Norway, along with the Skuas and Swordfish of *Furious*'s other squadrons. This operation, incidentally, was the first squadron-strength night attack undertaken by the FAA, a month before the now legendary Swordfish attack on the Italian Navy at Taranto. As an attack the Tromso raid proved to be only part-successful, with some aircraft failing to identify targets correctly and dropping their bombs well south of these, close to a petrol installation and some civilian houses. It was also costly, with almost half the crews failing to return. Yet again Esmonde had to lead the surviving crews back to Hatston for replacements and another intensive training session to weld his crews into a 'whole' squadron.

In mid-November 1940 he despatched all 825 Squadron's Observers to RAF Odiham in Hampshire for an Army co-operation course with No 110 Squadron RCAF, flying Westland Lysanders; while he remained to continue training his pilots and TAGs at Arbroath. In early December one Flight of the squadron was sent south to Lee-on-Solent to fit ASV aerials (R.3039/T.3040) to its Swordfish, while the remaining crews at Arbroath also modified their aircraft. For the rest of the month, and indeed January and February 1941, the squadron led a relatively peaceful life, mainly attending lectures on ASV theory and practice, though the weather conditions – icy temperatures and a two-feet thick carpet of snow everywhere – gave few opportunities for flying instruction. Most married officers brought their wives to live in the Seaforth Arms Hotel in Arbroath.

Having mentioned already that Eugene Esmonde's initial period in command of No 825 Squadron had not particularly endeared him to certain of his subordinates, due to his apparent desire to get to grips with the enemy despite any odds against success or survival; the views of another fellow officer aboard HMS *Furious* during 1940, a Paymaster, not directly under Esmonde's command and thereby possibly more objective in his opinion, may in part help to balance the impression Esmonde made on his fellow Messmates. Lieutenant-Commander (S) Geoffrey H. Slade, RN Retd recalls: 'He appeared to be just an ordinary average Naval officer – rather an unobtrusive personality and by no means what might be described as a "Naval Hearty". I considered him to be much more mature for his age than the rest of us, and a good deal maturer than a good number of those senior to him. I think his squadron, certainly the more junior and "rorty" members, held him in considerable awe, though he was by no means a martinet and just as well liked by the squadron ratings. He was certainly the complete aviation professional, which was why his squadron was such a well-ordered unit.

'His naval experience could not have been extensive at that time, as he only joined in 1939, much later than some of his subordinates, but when I knew him he had certainly adapted in a very short space of time and might well have been in the RN all his life. However, it could not have been easy for him. At that time *Furious* was commanded by a Captain who was by no means everyone's cup of tea, with a very 'regimental' (though most upright and honest) second-in-command, and Esmonde's life aboard must have been pretty difficult coping with these types, to whom flying of any kind was an anathema and naval flying something akin to a witch riding on a broomstick. I think Esmonde's strength lay actually in character, without being at all obvious, coupled with his tremendous professional expertise.'

On 26 February 1941 Esmonde and his squadron of six Swordfish were once more embarked aboard HMS *Furious*, sailed from Scapa Flow to anchor off Gourock on the river Clyde, where the carrier was loaded with some fifty Hawker Hurricane fighters which were to be transported to the RAF's receiving depot at Takoradi in the Gold Coast, West Africa, for onward transmission to the RAF firstline squadrons fighting in North Africa. No 825 Squadron's prime role for this journey was as an anti-submarine protection force, supplementing a naval escort of six destroyers (for the first stages) and HMS *Repulse* for the full journey. By the beginning of March all was ready and *Furious* set out, with 825's Swordfish crews undertaking regular clearance search patrols daily, sweeping the ocean waters around the naval force. On 6 March Esmonde left the deck of *Furious* in Swordfish 'A', with Lieutenant Cardew as the squadron's Senior Observer and Leading Airman Russell, at 1700 hrs for a clearance search – and got lost! Cardew's notes describe this unusual event:

> On the previous evening the Swordfish flying the search had had to ask for a D/F bearing at the end – strict W/T silence was in force, of course – and on landing its Observer, Sub-Lt Fraser, reported extraordinary weather conditions. Since Fraser and his pilot were relatively inexperienced, Esmonde and I decided we should undertake the search on the 6th. We found exactly the same conditions – a bank of cloud then storm; ten to fifteen minutes later a bank of cloud then calm; a bank of cloud then storm; a bank of cloud then calm. This continued all the way out to the limit of our search. Accurate navigation was quite impossible but I did my best and decided to trust in the beacon and the ASV to get us back to *Furious*. However, shortly after turning for home both aids packed up. When we got to where *Furious* should be there was nothing in sight and, furthermore, it was practically dark. We carried out a square search but found nothing – it was now fully dark.
>
> We did, however, pass over one of our screening destroyers which had been released to return to base, having reached the limits of its operational range. I noted its course and speed just in

case we had to return to it and ditch. Esmonde and I discussed our predicament and eventually decided to break W/T silence and request a D/F bearing. How very sweet it sounded when it came through, and what relief when the deck landing lights were switched on some ten minutes later as we circled *Furious*. In all my flying career I had never experienced such extreme changes of weather in such short intervals. During the latter half of this flight Esmonde was a great help in giving me confidence, helping me to analyse my navigation to try to find out where any mistakes might be. He was very different from the dogmatic pilot I had on the Trondheim raid. Possibly that was the first time he had ever been lost at night over a wide ocean with no possibility of reaching land, friendly or otherwise.

Cardew continued:

Furious had an uneventful journey to Takoradi, but due to her old age she was badly in need of a refit, and was losing more fresh water through leaky steam joints than she could make. Water, therefore, was severely rationed. On arrival off Takoradi on 20 March 1941 Esmonde and I, with LA Russell, flew to the RAF base to act as a liaison team. We were greeted by the CO and other senior officers who we noticed always kept to windward of us. After the usual pleasantries, they suggested that we might like a wash and brush-up – and 'perhaps a bath?' – before drinks and lunch. We leapt at this invitation and felt wonderful after when we changed into white uniform from our drab, sweaty khaki. It was not until the first flight of Hurricanes landed that afternoon with the six intrepid RAF pilots we'd brought with us that we understood. With our strict water rationing, and only salt water baths but no salt water soap, only the usual Lux etc – we stank to high Heaven! The smell in *Furious* when we re-embarked two days later was awful – but we soon got used to it! The fifty Hurricanes were all successfully landed by the six very brave RAF pilots, none of whom had ever taken off from a carrier before. They were ferried back to *Furious* in our Swordfish, a journey they did not greatly enjoy, particularly the deck landings.

On 22 March Esmonde rejoined *Furious* which then sailed to Freetown to collect mail, stores, and fresh water before pressing on to Gibraltar, and to wait for the next north-bound convoy. En route to Gibraltar 825's Swordfish continued their anti-submarine searches and patrols daily, with a slight diversion from routine on 29 March when all aircraft gave a formation flying exhibition-type 'display' over the convoy, both to bolster the convoy's morale and to show what the Fleet Air Arm could do. On arrival at Gibraltar three of 825 Squadron's ASV Swordfish and their trained crews were transferred to the *Ark Royal*; one aircraft with crew to each of the *Ark*'s three 'resident' squadrons.

Finally reaching home again, the remaining crews of the squadron were disembarked on 12 April, going temporarily to Campbelltown, but moving to Hatston five days later. Here, for the fourth time in the year of his command, Esmonde began quickly bringing 825 Squadron back to full fighting strength and training his latest batch of fresh replacement crews.

CHAPTER SIX

Send Her Victorious

Esmonde's latest reconstruction of 825 Squadron at Machrihanish, a grass airfield near Campbelltown, Argyll, and Hatston proved to be relatively brief. Replacement Swordfish were fairly easily obtainable, but fresh crews meant combing various sources for both experienced and inexperienced air crews. Among these newly joining 825 Squadron was Lieutenant Percy Gick, a very experienced pre-war naval pilot who had spent most of the war to date instructing naval crews in torpedo dropping from Sharks and Swordfish at Gosport, Abbotsinch, and Crail. Thoroughly bored with such non-active duties, Gick had made several requests for an operational post:

'After a lot of protest about this rather dull pastime (perhaps dull is not quite the right word; I was struck three times whilst in formation by some of my less able pupils), I was posted to join 825 Squadron, commanded by Eugene Esmonde, which was forming up on an old grass airfield near Campbelltown on the Mull of Kintyre. It was a nine-aircraft squadron of Swordfish. Esmonde, of course, led the first three; I as Senior Pilot led the next three; and 'Speed' Pollard the other three. 'Speed' [Lieutenant H.C.P. Pollard, RN] was quite a good pilot but was so named because in his speech he was *unbelievably* slow. We spent a few weeks there, trying to get the squadron into shape. Most of the pilots had been through my hands at Gosport, Abbotsinch or Crail and my impression was that everything I had tried to teach them they had entirely forgotten.'

Another member with previous experience was Lieutenant Colin Ennever, an Observer who had flown with Esmonde aboard HMS *Furious* during its recent return from Gibraltar. Given ten days' leave on disembarking from *Furious*, Ennever was picked up by Esmonde from Abbotsinch in a Swordfish and flown back to the squadron: 'Percy Gick had just come from the torpedo training school at Crail, Fife, and became the No 2 Flight commander, while Sub-Lieutenant Thompson, with a Sub-Lieutenant Parkinson, became commander of the third Flight. I was Squadron Observer and virtually 2nd i/c, although for all practical purposes Gick, slightly junior in pure seniority but an infinitely experienced pilot, would take over if required. Two Army officers were attached to Machrihanish to exercise us in army co-operation whilst the squadron worked up from the (then) grass runways. There was an officer in charge of the very small naval unit there, a Lieutenant-Commander 'Bog' Beard, and we messed and slept in the Machrihanish (golf) hotel. Once Esmonde and I were taken to the army HQ at Inverary to consult on training matters. We did not know where we were intended for an operation, but in hindsight it may have been Madagascar.'

On 17 May 1941 Esmonde led his squadron from Machrihanish to Hatston, where he received further orders to embark 825 Squadron aboard a new aircraft carrier, HMS *Victorious*, then anchored in Scapa Flow. The *Victorious*, the fifth RN ship to bear that proud name, had originally been ordered to be built in 1936 as one of four new aircraft carriers of a new class, based on the latest *Ark Royal* design, and having armoured hull, deck, and aircraft hangars. Its keel was laid on 4 May 1937, and *Victorious* was eventually launched on 14 September 1939 – just eleven days after the outbreak of war between Britain and Germany. The carrier was then forced to wait until 16 April 1941 before making its maiden voyage, having been officially commissioned on 29 March that year, and as her sea trials progressed the Admiralty decided that the first operational task for *Victorious* was to be a 'Carter Paterson' ferrying trip to Malta to deliver a consignment of crated Hurricane fighters to that besieged island.

Accordingly, her captain was ordered to be ready to sail from the River Clyde on 22 May 1941 in company with the cruiser *Repulse* and Troop Convoy WS8B, bound for Gibraltar. A hectic few weeks ensued for the ship's crew, embarking stores, ammunition, No 1800Z Flight, FAA (six Fairey Fulmar aircraft under the command of Lieutenant-Commander J.A.D. Wroughton, RN), and finally forty-eight crated Hurricanes. Once all was aboard the *Victorious* sailed on 15 May to Scapa Flow. Here, on 20 May, she took on board Esmonde's 825 Squadron of nine Swordfish.

To Percy Gick fell the heavy responsibility of moving the squadron aircraft, crews, kits and caboodle to the carrier at very short notice:

'Because I had come straight from teaching people to do torpedo attacks, Esmonde left that part of the training of the squadron to me, and I think it's fair to say that I actually had about three or four days with the chaps in the air to teach them how to do a co-ordinated attack with nine aircraft before we got a message that *within 48 hours* we had to join *Victorious* at Scapa Flow, ready to proceed to the Mediterranean. As Senior Pilot it was my job to organise, as far as I could see, practically anything, and I soon found out that *Victorious* was equipped to embark Albacores, but not Swordfish, and therefore had no spares whatsoever.

'Fortunately for me at that time, and I suppose for the squadron, my father had at one time been Director of Naval Stores, and therefore I knew well Mr Mahoney who was then in charge of air stores. I immediately rang him at the Admiralty and his comment was typical: "I will lay on a few aircraft. Let me know what you want and I'll have it at Scapa in twelve hours' time." To pass such an order over the 'phone would have been almost impossible, so I grabbed all the books we had, indicating what stores we would need, jumped into a Stringbag and flew down to London with them. Mahoney, quite typically, found out about this and had a car meet me at Northolt, and by the time I got back to Machrihanish the stores we needed had been landed in the Orkneys.

'I dropped in to Machrihanish for some fuel, went on to the Orkneys, kicked a few senior officers in the sump, and got some lighters organised to get the stores aboard *Victorious*. Back to Machrihanish and we got on with the rest of the problems. In due course the squadron took off and landed on board *Victorious*. The hangar was packed with Hurricanes destined for Malta. Six Fulmars operated from one end of the hangar, and we had to do our best in the other end.'

While these preparations and moves were taking place in northern Scotland, ominous events were also taking place across the North Sea, events which were to bring an abrupt change in the

Admiralty's intentions for *Victorious* among many other RN ships. German depredations of Allied merchant shipping, particularly in the Atlantic zones, by U-boats and surface ships were reaching a disastrously high peak by early 1941. Part of that success had been achieved by the 'Ugly Sisters' *Scharnhorst* and *Gneisenau*, two capital surface raiders based at Brest, which between them had sunk no less than twenty-two Allied ships between January and March 1941 – a gross of 115,622 tons. Their orders for that period had been to engage only unescorted merchant shipping and to avoid direct clashes with Royal Navy ships. Such was their success that the German naval hierarchy decided to exploit the contemporary favourable situation by launching *Operation Rheinbung* – literally, 'Rhine Exercise' – whereby two other capital ships, *Bismarck* and *Prinz Eugen* were to join forces with their Brest-based 'sisters' in plundering the Atlantic convoy routes, with the significant difference of bolder terms of reference i.e. that *Bismarck* and *Prinz Eugen* were given free rein to attack all forms of Allied shipping unless a 15-inch gunned battleship was present.

The *Bismarck* – the 'Pride of the German Navy' as Adolf Hitler dubbed it – was the largest, most powerful battleship built for the German Navy when it was launched at Hamburg on 14 February 1939 by Dorothea von Löwenfeld, grand-daughter of the 'original' Iron Chancellor. Nearly 800 feet long, and weighing almost 51,000 tons fully loaded, the *Bismarck* was a floating arsenal with eight 15-inch, twelve 5.9-inch, and sixteen 4.1-inch guns, apart from a host of smaller anti-aircraft weapons. On 2 April 1941 preparatory orders for *Rheinbung* were issued stating that in the next new moon period *Bismarck, Gneisenau,* and the 14,000 tons heavy cruiser *Prinz Eugen* were to rendezvous in the Atlantic for a co-ordinated offensive against Allied shipping. *Scharnhorst*, due to extensive boiler repairs being underway, would for the moment remain in Brest harbour.

This plan received a setback on 6 April when Flying Officer Kenneth Campbell of No 22 Squadron RAF, flying Bristol Beaufort N1016, 'X', attacked the *Gneisenau* in the early morning, his torpedo striking the ship near the stern and shattering a propeller shaft apart from flooding two engine rooms. Campbell died seconds later in a fury of anti-aircraft fire, and was later awarded a posthumous

Victoria Cross; but his target, *Gneisenau*, was still high and dry undergoing repairs eight months later.

A further, though less serious 'hiccup' to the initial plan came on 24 April, when a magnetic mine exploded close to the *Prinz Eugen*, damaging a coupling and necessitating a two-weeks' repair job. Thus, the earliest the force could now sail together was near the end of May 1941. Germany's naval commanders consulted together, debating whether to postpone *Rheinbung* to a much later date when either *Scharnhorst* or the massive, 52,600-ton *Tirpitz* became available for operations. In the end the head of Hitler's Navy, Grand Admiral Erich Raeder, decided against any form of postponement, and a starting date for *Operation Rheinbung* was confirmed as 18 May 1941. Two days prior to that date nine support ships sailed from French and Norwegian ports to take up their waiting positions, ready to give *Bismarck* and *Prinz Eugen* supplies of oil, ammunition, food and water to last at least three months; while elsewhere four weather ships were seaborne, ready to pass on the necessary meteorological data when needed. The scene was now set for what would prove to be an epic sea-air conflict.

In the afternoon of Sunday, 18 May *Prinz Eugen* left harbour for preliminary degaussing tests against magnetic mines, to be followed a little later by *Bismarck*, and as dusk approached both ships set course and began sailing to Arkona, a cape in northern Prussia, to rendezvous with a minesweeper flotilla and two destroyers, reaching this point in the morning of 19 May. Only then, at noon, did *Bismarck*'s captain, Ernst Lindemann, tell his crew on the ship's loudspeaker system of the ship's orders – a three months' cruise of the Atlantic to destroy Allied shipping. Continuing their course all that day and night, the force passed through the Fehmarn Belt, then the Great Belt, picking up another destroyer en route, and eventually northwards along the Norwegian coast on a zig-zag course to avoid possible Allied submarines. Then, just before 9 am on 21 May, the main pair of ships turned to starboard and entered Korsfjord* and took pilots aboard who took *Bismarck* to Grimstad fjord, just south of Bergen,

---

* Now titled Krossfjord.

and *Prinz Eugen* to Kalvanes Bay north-west.

Here *Prinz Eugen* necessarily began re-oiling from a tanker, with orders to be ready to sail that evening, but *Bismarck*, despite having already burned off some 1000 tons of her fuel, did *not* replenish her tanks – in the hindsight of later events, an ill-judged, indeed fateful decision.

The movement of the huge ships throughout their journey to Norway had not gone unnoticed by a series of Allied sympathisers in German-occupied territories en route, and intelligence of the sea force had begun to reach Britain. At Scapa Flow lay the British Home Fleet commanded by Admiral Sir John Tovey, whose new flagship, *King George V*, lay moored off Flotta. The news of the German ships' apparent imminent departure from their harbours was not new to Tovey, but their actual whereabouts on the morning of 21 May was as yet unknown to him. Nevertheless, he had already given orders for various RN ships to take up stations in the Denmark Straits on the off-chance.

Then, around noon, two pilots of the RAF's photo-reconnaissance unit at Wick, Flying Officer C.A.S. Greenhill, DFC and Pilot Officer Michael – 'Babe' – Suckling, took off in PRU-modified Spitfires with orders to recce the Norwegian coast. Suckling, after refuelling at Sumburgh, set course for Bergen, made his landfall south of Sogne Fjord, and began photographing shipping in Hjelte Fjord, and the Herlo and Flatoen aircraft bases. He next spotted and photographed:

' ... one *Hipper*-class cruiser, one destroyer, and four MVs anchored ten miles west of Bergen. I then did a run over Bergen and while doing so saw what I took to be another *Hipper*-class cruiser and four MVs anchored at eastern end of Fiord, five miles south of Bergen. Photographed these and returned immediately to Wick. Photographs showed the second cruiser to be a *Bismarck*-class battleship.'* Suckling's photographs were swiftly shown to Tovey and then rushed to the Admiralty and RAF Coastal Command headquarters in Northwood, Middlesex. Tovey acted immediately, without awaiting further instructions from the Admiralty and,

---

* Flying Officer Michael Frank Suckling was killed on a PRU sortie over La Pallice on 21 July 1941.

when the *Victorious* returned to Scapa Flow after a brief exercise in mid-afternoon, signalled the carrier's Captain Henry Bovell to report to the flagship, where Tovey asked Bovell whether his Swordfish (825 Squadron) were able to undertake a torpedo strike against the German battleships. Bovell summoned Eugene Esmonde and the carrier's Flight Operations Officer, Commander H.C. Ranald, and all three agreed such an operation might be possible, despite the acknowledged inexperience of many of the squadron's air crews.

By early evening, however, weather conditions had deteriorated, with heavy sea mists and driving rain, thereby preventing any further aerial reconnaissance over Bergen. Admiral Tovey could only guess whether the German ships were still in the Norwegian fiord, or whether they had already set sail northwards with the aim of breaking into the open Atlantic via Icelandic waters. By 9 pm he had ordered HMS *Hood*, *Prince of Wales*, and six destroyers to sail from the Flow to take up waiting positions south-west of Iceland to cover the sea gaps Iceland-Greenland and Iceland-Faroes. About midnight, with the *Hood* leading, this force eased out of the Hoxa gate and set course for their designated battle stations. It was fated to be the mighty *Hood*'s ultimate voyage.

Tovey's fears were, in fact, well justified because before 8 pm that same evening *Bismarck* weighed anchor, turned north, joined up with her destroyer escort, then picked up station with the waiting *Prinz Eugen*, steamed up Hjeltefjord and the Fedjeosen, swung to port past the Skerries, and entered the open sea heading due north to the Arctic Ocean.

Early next morning Admiral Tovey was still without confirmation of the precise location of the German ships; an RAF bombing raid the night before against Korsfjord and Bergen had been baffled by weather conditions and seen nothing of their target. Finally, at 4.30 pm a Martin Maryland twin-engined target-towing aircraft, piloted by Lieutenant-Noel Goddard, took off from the Shetlands and in appalling cloud conditions reached Korsfjord and Grimstad, found no sign of enemy ships anywhere, and returned to base at 7.45 pm to report their findings. Tovey, accordingly signalled *Victorious*, four cruisers and six destroyers to be ready to sail by 10.15 pm, at the same time ordering further reinforcements for his already seaborne 'watchdogs' off Iceland and in the Denmark Straits. Thus, in the late evening of 22 May 1941, the hunt was on.

The following two days were filled with incident – and tragedy. In the evening of 23 May the RN cruisers *Norfolk* and *Suffolk* got their first sight of the German ships as these headed south-westwards between Iceland and Greenland, skirting the vast pack ice barrier off Greenland's south-east coastline. Both cruisers immediately took up the role of trailers, keeping behind but in pace with the German force and radioing their intelligence to the other RN ships in the chase. At 0600 hours on 24 May the *Hood*, now at some 25,000 yards range from the *Bismarck*, began to engage with its guns. Within four minutes of devastating exchange of gunfire, which had already started a fire amidships on the boat deck of the *Hood*, one of *Bismarck*'s shells penetrated the *Hood*'s deck between centre and stern, plunging into the ship's innards, then exploded; detonating two magazines and literally tearing the huge ship in two. The shattered sections of the *Hood* slid rapidly into the ocean depths, taking with them the entire ship's crew of 1419 men with the exception of one midshipman and two ratings – the only three survivors.

Bismarck and *Prinz Eugen* then gave their undivided attentions to the *Prince of Wales*, hitting her with four 15-inch and three 8-inch shells and making her break off the engagement and retire under cover of a smoke screen. Nevertheless, before leaving the fight *Prince of Wales* had managed to inflict three positive hits on the *Bismarck*; the most serious of these having struck the port bow on the waterline, penetrating two oil tanks, and exiting through the starboard bow without exploding. Sea water flooded in to the ruptured oil tanks and released a steady stream of oil into the sea; while the shell had also smashed the suction valves, thereby cutting off the supply of 1000 tons of oil to the engines. With its bow now down by several degrees, and a list to port of nine degrees, the *Bismarck* was forced to reduce speed to 28 knots maximum.

On assessing the damage, and his deteriorating fuel position, Admiral Gunther Lütjens, the German Fleet commander, sent a signal back to Germany announcing the damage and his intention to return *Bismarck* to St Nazaire for dockyard repairs. Then, gradually losing speed, *Bismarck* began altering her course towards the south – and unknowingly set her bows in a direction which would close the range between berself and Admiral Tovey's force of *King George V*, *Victorious*, and others at that time sailing at top speed almost due westwards towards the German force.

In the late afternoon of 24 May Admiral Tovey ordered *Victorious* and four cruisers to split off from their course to proceed to a position within 100 miles of *Bismarck*'s expected location, from where the carrier could launch an air strike by the Swordfish of 825 Squadron. Though it was unlikely that aerial torpedoes would actually sink such a heavily armoured ship, it was hoped that they might at least slow the German ship, thus allowing the main naval force to close and engage. By 10 pm that evening the *Victorious* was still some 120 miles away from *Bismarck*, rather more than an ideal operating range for heavily-laden Swordfish, but weather conditions were getting worse, with a rising north-westerly wind churning up a 32-feet swell and covering the carrier in spasmodic deluges of sea spray and scudding rain. The light would only last until about midnight at best, meaning a return in the dark for the Swordfish crews, and any postponement of take-off would only exacerbate the problems.

Accordingly, shortly after 10 pm the order came down from the bridge for 825 Squadron to go. The first Swordfish, '5A', was piloted by Eugene Esmonde, with Colin Ennever in its Observer's seat and Pilot Officer Parker as TAG, and as he staggered off the windswept carrier deck the remaining eight aircraft quickly followed suit, eventually forming up as best they could with Esmonde's leading aircraft as he set a course of 225 degrees at a speed of some 85 knots. The ensuing action by 825 Squadron against *Bismarck* is best described in the words of Percy Gick, leader of No 2 Flight:

'Only after we sailed were we told of the *Bismarck* panic. My problem was how to get all nine aircraft serviceable, with torpedoes on, and the pilots briefed on how we were to attack. As we steamed full speed towards the *Bismarck* to intercept, it was becoming abundantly clear that we were going to run out of daylight. I had always been crazy about operating at night – it struck me as the only sensible thing to do because the opposition couldn't see you so well and they were therefore less likely to shoot you down.

'I'd done my deck landings at night because I had done some of the initial trials in the old *Ark Royal* before the war. Esmonde, I think, had done two.* The rest of the pilots had done very little nightflying and not one of them a night deck landing. When I was asked whether or not we should attempt to attack at such a time that we would arrive back after dark, I gave as my advice that probably half the aircraft would get back on board intact, and if the rest of the air crews couldn't make it at least they could ditch and get picked up by a destroyer. In due course we were launched. In the back of my aircraft I had as TAG a delightful man, Petty Officer (A) L.D. Sayer, and my Observer was Sub-Lieutenant V.K. Norfolk – known as 'Duke' – who was a brilliant Observer and a genius with the old Mk 2 ASV radar.

'As we approached the *Bismarck* Norfolk quietly shouted down through the (*speaking*) tube, "She's on the port bow and I've got an idea I can see someone shadowing her". A little later he confirmed that he had the *Bismarck* as a big blip on the port bow, a slightly smaller one on the starboard bow and, some few minutes later, something even smaller roughly ahead.

'We were flying in three sub-Flights, each in a Vic of three, and the three Flights in a Vic. Looking across at Esmonde's aircraft it was abundantly clear that Colin Ennever's set was not working as well and he had nothing. Of course, we had no radio communication then. I had to bring my sub-Flight ahead to attract Esmonde's back cockpit's attention so that Norfolk could make hand signals to indicate to Colin Ennever that the enemy was on the port bow. To this day I don't know what happened to the set in Esmonde's aircraft but apparently the port aerial wasn't working and the starboard was, and all Colin could see was HMS *Sheffield* on the starboard bow. In spite of all our efforts Esmonde peeled off and we lost our gorgeous height in attacking the *Sheffield*. Fortunately, everybody recognised the ship and no torpedoes were dropped; we tried to reform and climbed away. As we did so on our starboard beam we saw first the coastguard cutter *Modoc*, and a bit later the

---

* In fact, Esmonde had done many more night deck landings, but only years before during his RAF/FAA service – Author.

Bismarck on our starboard bow. Swordfish with torpedoes on did not climb easily and it was quite clear that if we were going to do a successful attack we had to get a bit of altitude in order to pick up some speed, and as a squadron we started to climb away. Our climbing speed at this time was about 75 knots.

'*Bismarck* sighted us and opened fire. Her fire was astonishingly accurate for range and looked nasty because there were great balls of black where shells exploded ahead of us.* It was not until years later that I discovered that the Germans could not believe that any aircraft would ever fly at less than 100 knots, and their fire control system when firing at us was at its lowest possible setting, and therefore all bursting harmlessly ahead. Eventually Esmonde peeled off with his sub-Flight and went in to the attack. Obviously, if we all went in from the same direction she would turn in to us, so I carried on still climbing a little and then levelled off.

'My problem was that Esmonde having started his attack meant that unless I got in reasonably soon she would comb his torpedoes and then mine. By this time "Speed' Pollard had also peeled off and I lost sight of him because there was a lot of misty cloud around. So I decided we must go in. As we got within a few thousand yards I saw Esmonde drop his torpedoes and pull out. It was clear that *Bismarck* had plenty of time to comb his torpedoes and then turn in to mine. So I pulled away and dived straight down to sea level, and then turned back hoping to get in unobserved.

'There was hell of a sea running and I really got down on the surface and kept losing sight of her behind the waves. On my left Pat Jackson† was doing the same, but on my right Bill Garthwaite**, a very recently qualified student of mine, who throughout his distinguished career in the FAA during the war seemed to be quite convinced that nobody would ever shoot him down, went in quite steadily and, when we were sighted, drew all the fire. His Observer, Anthony Gillingham†† commented

---

* Even at this, some four miles' range, one shell ripped away one of Esmonde's ailerons. Author.

† Sub-Lieutenant D.P.B. Jackson, RNVR.

** Lieutenant (A) W.F.C. Garthwaite, RNVR, now, Sir William.

†† Sub-Lieutenant (A) W.A. Gillingham, RNVR.

afterwards: "He didn't mind the stuff going above him and below him, but it was those beastly little balls of fire that nipped in *between* the wings that upset him".

'I like to think that I got to the right range, but she was hell of a big ship and I have a horrid feeling I may have dropped a little too early. Anyhow, I did, and as I dropped Bill and Pat did so also and we pulled and turned away. By this time there was hell of a lot of fireworks going on, but my dear Observer had brought with him a very expensive camera and was determined to get some pictures, and insisted that I should turn this way and that whilst he photographed the ship.

'Frankly, I thought the whole thing terribly unhealthy and stupid, and in fact it very nearly was because when eventually he was satisfied and I got down on the water and flew away, *Bismarck* did what I regarded as one of the most unsporting things of all, which was to lob 15-inch shells at us. These caused great inconvenience because one of them landed ahead of us and I flew through the splash. The whole aircraft gained about thirty feet in altitude, and the only comment came out of Sayer during the whole four hours' flight when he said, "Goddam! Some rotten sod's knocked the bottom out of my house". The splash had literally ripped the fabric off the bottom part of his cockpit, and he was sitting gazing into fresh air for the rest of the trip back.

'Our next problem was to find the carrier. This presented some difficulties, but the Captain (Bless him ...) decided to break silence and give us a quick call on which we could come home. As we got back in the dark we saw the lights of the rest of the aircraft. Esmonde landed on first. I followed him. As I taxied up to the forward end of the flight deck the bows dipped and a dirty great sea came over and saltwater flew all over the aircraft. Sayer spoke again, "Ah well, that bloody hole's come in handy". Esmonde and I were quite convinced that the other aircraft had crashed, but one by one they came on in some sort of shambles, got onto the deck, and were got ahead of the barrier. I think it was Bill Garthwaite who hit the deck with a resounding thud, bounced into the air, quickly slammed his throttle open and went round again. Eventually the whole lot got aboard with incredibly little damage either from the gunfire or the landings.'

The actual attack of 825 Squadron's Swordfish was made with eight of the original nine which set out – the ninth returning to the carrier early in the sortie with mechanical problems – while Eugene Esmonde's actual torpedo attack was described by his Observer, Colin Ennever:

'The first shells were thrown against us and we had to abandon sub-Flight tight formation at a distance of about four miles. As we neared *Bismarck* the equivalent of pom-pom with tracer alarmingly seemed to pass through the mainplanes. Although we didn't know until landing, our starboard lower mainplane was ripped and holed badly. I called out to Esmonde via voice pipe at one-quarter and one-half mile distances until he considered position and sang out "Going down". I tapped the air gunner on his shoulder and gave him the sign and we buttoned on our breast parachutes – more against splinters than otherwise. Esmonde made a perfect drop at 800 yards or so and turned down wind to the left. As we came round Parker was firing his K-gun madly at the *Bismarck* – most cheering. The *Bismarck* seemed to be swinging to starboard or away from us. At a few feet above the waves we seemed to be lower than their fire. Passing the bow, I saw a column of water jump funnel high on the starboard amidships side and black smoke issue from her funnel – a definite hit – followed by a smaller water column on the port side. I instructed our air gunner to wireless "One definite hit, one probable. Returning". Gick from the anti-aircraft mêlée attacked from starboard, probably unseen, and it may have been his drop.

'We joined four other aircraft, one followed at a distance, and then, having time now to do some navigation, wheeled them about 30 degrees left. The weather was calmer but almost dark. I conferred with Esmonde on obtaining a radio D/F bearing, i.e. breaking wireless silence in the vicinity of the fleet. He agreed, and on receipt we wheeled another 25 degrees to left. It was now dark with visibility uncertain. After twenty-five minutes Esmonde instructed me to send a message asking for a searchlight into the air. It was cheering to see the fleet ahead with this. After landing and debriefing it was probable we would do another attack at daylight, about 5 am. Going to bed clothed, I next remember Esmonde standing over me saying, "It's 7 am. The others were sent off on a recce at 6 am. I didn't call you as our mainplane is too damaged and under repair. We'll go off when they return".

'Meanwhile, the shadowers had lost the *Bismarck*. Two Swordfish did not return. They were the youngest and probably the least experienced in Observers and TAGs*, and it may have been a combination of the large variation of the compasses and the difficulties of the then new type of radio set which, because of its many knobs, was known as the "Wurlitzer". One aircraft, with Sub-Lieutenant Jackson (pilot) and Berrill (Observer) crew, were rescued some ten days later from a lifeboat, complete with water and sailing gear, which they had landed alongside, and were taken to Reykjavik. We remaining did another recce in the afternoon to north-east but without success.'

Apart from further reconnaissances flown by 825's Swordfish on 25 and 26 May, and some anti-submarine patrols, the carrier *Victorious* took no further part in the death of the *Bismarck*. Of the torpedoes launched at the German battleship by 825 Squadron's crews, only one was known to have struck the target, and this hit *Bismarck* in its armoured belt just below the waterline. The explosion blasted upwards rather than inwards – 'barely scratching the paint' as one of the ship's crew remarked later – though its blast threw a Chief Boatswain against the ship's aircraft hangar wall and fractured his skull (*Bismarck*'s first fatal casualty) and three Luftwaffe airmen received broken legs from the same detonation wave.

By one of those strange coincidences which occur in wartime, Eugene was not the only Esmonde involved in the hunt of the *Bismarck*.

On 25 May, the day after 825 Squadron's torpedo assault, a force of six *Tribal*-class destroyers, commanded by Captain Phillip Vian, engaged the *Bismarck* shortly before midnight. Four of these destroyers were from the Fourth Destroyer Flotilla, *Cossack*, *Maori*, *Sikh*, and *Zulu*; the latter being commanded by Commander H.R. Graham, and its engineer officer being Lieutenant-Commander Witham Esmonde. By a further coincidence, at the moment when

---

* In fact, Sub-Lieutenant David Berrill was an Observer with reasonably long operational experience, having survived several crashes and a ditching on operations in 1940-41. *Author.*

Swordfish of 825 Squadron waiting to leave HMAC *Victorious* to attack the *Bismarck*, May 1941.

Swordfish crash aboard HMAC *Victorious* on return from reconnaissance for the *Bismarck*, May 1941.

Eugene Esmonde was leading his Swordfish in to attack the *Bismarck*, less than twenty miles away a convoy was heading towards Britain and aboard one ship was Eugene's twin brother James. A qualified mining engineer, James was returning from the Gold Coast of West Africa.*

It fell to another force of Swordfish to seal *Bismarck*'s fate. At 7.10 pm in the evening of 26 May, the first of 15 Swordfish, led by Lieutenant-Commander Tim Coode, took off from the carrier *Ark Royal* and just before 9 pm began a series of individual torpedo attacks against the *Bismarck* despite thick clouds and mist obscuring visibility above 800 feet altitude. All returned to their carrier, although three crashed on landing and became write-offs, while one Swordfish had sustained 175 separate holes from the battleship's fierce anti-aircraft fire. Nevertheless, the crews could claim at least two strikes; one of these hitting the ship's armoured 'belt' and causing little damage, but the other torpedo, striking starboard aft, had breached and flooded the steering gear compartments and jammed the ship's rudders at 15-degrees to port.

Unable to steer a predictable course now, the *Bismarck* was helpless to evade or escape from the closing ring of Royal Navy hounds approaching for the kill. The end came on 27 May when *Bismarck* was relentlessly pounded to rubble by its tormentors, and at 10.40 am, with sea valves opened and her scuttling charges exploded, the Pride of the German Navy turned completely over and slid into its ocean grave. Of *Bismarck*'s full crew complement of 2287 men, only 107 were eventually retrieved from the sea.

The carrier *Victorious* did not remain to witness or participate in the final kill, but set course and returned to the Clyde, where she embarked her former consignment of crated Hurricane fighters earmarked for ferry to Malta. 825 Squadron's part in the *Bismarck* episode was later officially recognised and rewarded. Eugene Esmonde, as leader, was awarded a Distinguished Service Order (DSO), Percy Gick a Distinguished Service Cross (DSC), Sub-

---

* At that time, apart from Owen who was serving as a Pilot Officer with the RAF, Eugene's sister Carmel was a member of the WAAF, and his youngest brother 'Paddy' had followed in their father's footsteps and was an officer in the RAMC.

825 Sqn personnel decorated for their part in the *Bismarck* affair. From left; Lt P.D. Gick; Lt-Cdr E. Esmonde; Sub-Lt V.K. Norfolk (Gick's Observer); PO L.D. Sayer (Gick's TAG); L/A A.L. 'Ginger' Johnson. Taken aboard HMAC *Ark Royal*.

Lieutenant 'Duke' Norfolk a DSC, while Gick's TAG, Petty Officer Les Sayer and TAG, Leading Airman A.L. 'Ginger' Johnson each received a Distinguished Service Medal (DSM). Esmonde's DSO was officially promulgated in the *London Gazette* dated 16 September 1941.

By 31 May *Victorious* was ready to sail and, in company with HMS *Norfolk* and *Neptune*, left port at midnight in the wake of Convoy W58X for the first stage to Gibraltar. 825 Squadron's daily protective role was in the main a series of anti-submarine 'watch and ward' patrols in the convoy area, but on 4 June its Swordfish spotted and halted a German supply ship, *Gonzenheim*. Ironically, this vessel had been waiting to rendezvous with the *Bismarck*, some 200 miles north of the Azores. Realising that its war career was over, *Gonzenheim*'s crew scuttled their ship before a Royal Navy boarding party could reach it, and its 63-men crew were taken aboard *Victorious* as prisoners of war. Five days later the carrier linked up with the RN's Force H, which included *Ark Royal*, and on 11 June the combined force reached Gibraltar.

Once in port the *Ark Royal* embarked twenty-four of the Hurricanes from *Victorious* in order to ease the latter's space problems, and on 13 June, escorted by seven destroyers, both carriers left the Rock and sailed to a point just south of the Balearic Islands, from where they flew off a total of forty-seven Hurricanes, all but two of these actually managing to reach Malta safely. Returning again to Gibraltar Esmonde, to his dismay, received an order to transfer his 825 Squadron from *Victorious* to *Ark Royal*. Despite his protestation that his unit had been specially trained for a forthcoming Army co-operation operation, his orders were confirmed, and on 16 June he flew his Swordfish onto *Ark Royal*. In doing so he relieved the *Ark*'s former resident 820 Squadron FAA, which was transferred to *Victorious* and left Gibraltar with that carrier on 19 June bound for the United Kingdom.

CHAPTER SEVEN

The Ark

The transfer of Esmonde's 825 Squadron from *Victorious* to the *Ark Royal*, in spite of his protests, meant yet another semi-dissembling of the unit. Several air crew personnel were at the same time shifted from 825 to 820 Squadron, fortunately many of these being junior, recently-arrived men; while one sub-Flight of 825 was detached to Malta to bolster that beleaguered island's air-strike capabilities.

Ark Royal, commanded by Captain L.E.H. Maund, had a long and distinguished history already. Its 'grandparent', the very first *Ark Royal*, had been built at Deptford by Sir Walter Raleigh's private order, and in the custom of the period bore its owner's name, thus *Ark Raleigh*. However, before its launching in 1587 the Crown had taken her over and renamed the ship *Ark Royal*. With her displacement of almost 1500 tons, she became the flagship of Lord Howard of Effingham, the Lord High Admiral of England, and took a leading part in the destruction of the Spanish Armada. Later rebuilt, and renamed *Anne Royal* (after the queen of James I), she was wrecked in 1636.

The second *Ark Royal* resulted from an Admiralty decision in late 1913 to drastically redesign a tramp steamer, still in frame, in the Blyth Company's shipbuilding yard, into a 'seaplane carrier'. Named *Ark Royal*, this converted tramp was launched in September 1914 and commissioned for service on 9 December. Seeing gallant operational service in the Gallipoli campaign and elsewhere during World War One, the 'carrier' remained named *Ark Royal* until 1935 when the Admiralty decided to have built a truly modern aircraft carrier to bear the name. Accordingly, the second *Ark Royal* was retitled as *Pegasus*, and was to see non-operational use in the 1939-45 conflict.

The new (third) *Ark Royal*'s keel was laid on 16 September 1935, and some eighteen months later, on 13 April 1937, she was launched from her Birkenhead yard by Lady Maud Hoare. Costing almost two and a half million pounds to build, this latest bearer of the name *Ark Royal* boasted nine decks in all, including an 800 feet long flight deck on top, with three double-decker aircraft lifts from the vast internal hangars to the iron flat-top flying surface. Initially embarking a crew complement of 1575 men, she could accommodate up to sixty of the contemporary FAA aircraft designs.

The *Ark* was officially commissioned on 16 November 1938, was completed by 16 December, and commenced her trials in the Clyde; while the first aircraft to be flown onto her gleaming new flight deck were the Swordfish of No 820 Squadron FAA on 12 January 1939, these having been transferred from the carrier *Courageous*, and led in by the unit commander Lieutenant-Commander A.C.G. Ermen, RN.

Once her 'chicks' had been stowed below *Ark Royal* set off to the Mediterranean for her maiden cruise, returning to the Home Fleet in April 1939. By then the imminence of war with Hitler's Germany had become apparent to all but the obtuse, and on 31 August 1939 the Home Fleet quietly put to sea, including the *Ark Royal*, to patrol the northern exit waters from the North Sea to the open Atlantic between the Shetlands and Norway – in effect, the carrier's first 'war' patrol. Next day one of her Swordfish brood forcelanded and sank in a Norwegian fiord, but its crew managed to reach shore in a rubber dinghy. Hastily flown to Bergen by their 'hosts', the crew were equally quickly shipped back to Britain – had they remained in Norway beyond 48 hours they might well have been interned in neutral custody and thereby become the *Ark*'s first war casualties.

Minutes after 11 am on 3 September 1939 the *Ark Royal*, along with every other RN vessel, received the Admiralty cipher signal 'Total Germany' – the real war had started. Three weeks later, on 26 September, Blackburn Skuas of the *Ark*'s No 803 Squadron clashed with three Dornier 18 flying boats shadowing the carrier, and one Dornier, Werke No 731 of 2 Staffel/Kü.Fl.GR.506, was shot down on the sea by Lieutenant B.S. McEwen in Skua L2873 – the first naval air 'kill' of the war. At 1420 hrs the same day a Heinkel 111 dive-bombed the carrier from low cloud cover, its 2000lb bomb narrowly missing its target by some 90 feet. The

Heinkel's pilot, Adolf Francke, returned to base and reported, making no claim for sinking the ship, but the German propaganda machinery immediately proclaimed the *Ark Royal* as sunk. Francke, awarded an Iron Cross and promoted for his 'feat', suffered the ridicule of his fellow fliers, but for many months thereafter German radios kept up a mocking chorus of 'Where is the *Ark Royal?*'

The carrier's answer was to be a continuing series of operations ranging from hunting the ill-fated *Graf Spee* in the south Atlantic in late 1939, to Narvik in May 1940, action at Oran two months later, escorting convoys through the Mediterranean throughout July 1940 to November 1941, with 'sideshow' operations such as its vital part in the trapping of the *Bismarck* in May 1941.

During the majority of those operations *Ark Royal* was to endure intensive air attacks and submarine onslaughts – particularly during its long sojourn in the dangerous waters of the Mediterranean – and yet the carrier was never damaged. Its only war casualties were from the various FAA squadrons embarked aboard her as these both defended their base from Luftwaffe and Regia Aeronautica attacks, and undertook many offensive sorties against a variety of enemy targets.

By June 1941, when Eugene Esmonde led his 825 Squadron's Swordfish aboard the *Ark Royal*, the carrier was a component of the Royal Navy's H Force – the prime naval force in the Mediterranean zone of operations then. The Force's main roles were convoy protection over the Gibraltar-Malta-Egypt routes, and the conveyance of Hurricanes, Blenheims, and other aircraft reinforcements to Malta. *Ark Royal* arrived back in Gibraltar on 29 May after its vital part in the sinking of the *Bismarck*, and in company with *Victorious* set out on a delivery operation in early June, flying off forty-seven Hurricanes for Malta between them on 10 June. On its return to Gibraltar again *Ark Royal* embarked Esmonde's 825 Squadron, thereby bringing the carrier's air arm up to a strength of three Swordfish squadrons (Nos 810, 818, 825), and two Fulmar fighter squadrons (Nos 807 and 808); a maximum of slightly more than fifty operational aircraft. In July 1941 No 818 was replaced by 816 Squadron (nine Swordfish), while in September 1941 No 812 Squadron (12 Swordfish) replaced No 810 Squadron aboard the carrier. Other air cover for Force H during most of that year was provided variously by one or more of three other carriers, *Argus*, *Furious*, and/or *Victorious*.

The date on which Esmonde joined the *Ark* left him with little time for normal working-up with the ship for his squadron, but his task was eased by the reunion with several old friends of his early FAA days who were now in the crew of the *Ark Royal*, including Lieutenant-Commander Patrick Stringer, now the *Ark*'s Flight Deck Officer, and the carrier's Commander Operations, Commander Wolf Bentinck. The Swordfishes' role was to be anti-submarine protection patrols around the carrier when at sea primarily, though additional reconnaissance sorties *et al* might be required on occasion. When employed on carriage of RAF aircraft and air crews destined for Malta, Esmonde's former RAF service enabled him to converse and mix on closer terms with the RAF personnel than most 'pure' RN officers, although relations between the two Services aboard the *Ark* were always congenial – each fully appreciating the other's problems and efforts. The system for embarking, carrying, and eventually despatching RAF Hurricanes to Malta via aircraft carrier had, by early 1941, begun to be a fairly routine business for the RN crews. In the main, such aircraft were conveyed from the United Kingdom by the carrier *Furious* as far as Gibraltar, then manually transferred from the *Furious* to the *Ark Royal* via a wooden ramp devised by Captain Maund. One Hurricane pilot, Fred Etchells, who was transported with No 249 Squadron RAF in this manner said of his experience:

'We believed we were heading for Singapore and our twenty-four Hurricane Is, tropicalised and fitted with long range tanks, had been dismantled, taken aboard *Furious* at Liverpool, reassembled, and crammed into a hangar below the flight deck. I had not heard of Hurricanes taking off from aircraft carriers and was very intrigued. Greenock was our first port of call, where we took on fresh water and were again away within an hour or so. Then Gibraltar, where we moored at the dockside on to HMS *Ark Royal* (which by then had been 'sunk' by Dr Goebbels about three times ...), and shortly after arrival we pilots helped push our Hurricanes over a bridge of planks joining the two ships.

'As soon as this chore was completed *Ark Royal* cast off and headed west into the Atlantic (to fool observers in local trawlers etc

HM Aircraft Carrier *Ark Royal*.

Swordfish 'landing on'.

who reported all shipping movements to the Germans – or so we were told). In the middle of the night a sharp turn through 180 degrees and through the Straits of Gibraltar – briefing next day for the first leg of our flight (which was to be Malta for refuelling and rest) – packing kit into ammunition recesses and any odd spots in the fuselage we could find – then all set for the off at dawn.

'All twenty-four of our Hurricanes were tightly crowded at the "blunt end" of the carrier and I remember my almost complete disbelief at the impossibly short runway. *Ark Royal* then opened her throttles and headed into wind at something like 30 knots, which meant a further 30 mph by the aircraft would give us the 60 mph needed for takeoff. Conscious of the heavily laden state of my machine, I was grateful for the great height of the flight deck above sea level, which had made me quite dizzy when looking over the side earlier in the journey. It meant no immediate necessity to climb until adequate flying speed was gained. I still recall the joy of seeing the aircraft in front of me becoming safely airborne before reaching the end of the flight deck at the "sharp end". Many of our pilots swore they bent their throttle levers to ensure maximum revs!'

Esmonde's 825 Squadron was to remain aboard *Ark Royal* for some five months, June to November 1941, during which period it underwent a series of various operational activities. Flying Swordfish '5A' during June-July, and aircraft '4A' thereafter, Eugene took his fair share of the daily routine and anti-submarine and general reconnaissance chore flights; in the interim continuing to bring the lesser experienced crews up to higher standards of carrier flying techniques. On 21 July *Operation Substance* was begun – a large Malta-bound convoy for which, in addition to Force H, the *Nelson*, *Arethusa*, *Edinburgh*, and *Manchester* were loaned from the Home Fleet. Leaving Gibraltar on that date, the convoy met determined opposition from the Italian air force from early on 23 July, and further harassment from a force of Italian MTBs. *Manchester*, *Firedrake*, and *Fearless* were each torpedoed; the *Fearless* being so badly damaged it was sunk by other Allied ships, while *Manchester* managed to limp back to Gibraltar, and *Firedrake* just contrived to stay afloat. Air attacks were eventually warded off by the guns and aircraft of *Ark Royal* and other escorts, and at

(Right) 'Booted' Swordfish (i.e. fitted with floats) flying over the rain catchments on Gilbraltar.

(Below) Eugene Esmonde (left) with Surgeon-Commander Williams aboard the *Ark Royal*.

midnight on 24 July Lieutenant William Garthwaite led six Swordfish – two from each of the *Ark*'s three squadrons – off the carrier's deck, narrowly avoiding collision with the masts of *Repulse* sailing ahead of the *Ark* – and flew these to Malta where they were to supplement the island's anti-shipping strike forces. Next day the convoy was split into two formations, with one continuing to Malta with the vital supplies, while *Ark Royal* escorted the damaged *Firedrake* back to Gibraltar safely.

Escort duties by the *Ark* continued through August 1941, though these were interrupted on occasion for 'one-off' airborne actions. On 24 August, for example, Esmonde, piloting Swordfish '4A', with Colin Ennever as his Observer, led an incendiary bombing attack on the cork woods at Tempio, Sardinia during the early morning hours. Next morning Esmonde was again airborne, this time leading a tight formation of all three of the *Ark*'s Swordfish squadrons over Valencia and the Spanish coastal towns – a display specially requested by the British Consul to show that the *Ark Royal* was still very much alive in spite of the continuing propaganda emerging from Germany.

That same evening Esmonde and Ennever flew an unscheduled flight, searching for the crew of Swordfish '4G' which had failed to return from a reconnaissance sortie. He eventually spotted the crew – Sub-Lieutenants Houston and Turner – some thirty miles from the *Ark* and directed their safe rescue from the sea. On another occasion the Swordfish undertook a night bombing raid against Alghero aerodrome on the west coast of Sardinia, obtaining direct hits on several hangars and buildings.

On 24 September *Operation Halberd* commenced; a large troop (some 2000-plus) and supplies convoy of nine ships, heavily protected by *Nelson, Rodney, Prince of Wales, Ark Royal*, five cruisers, and eighteen destroyers – a formidable array of Royal Navy strength. Within forty-eight hours of leaving Gibraltar the *Halberd* force came under close attack from Italian air torpedo-bombers. Two of the attackers were shot down before getting within range of the convoy, while another pair sheered away from the intense gun barrage put up by the escort ships. The rest pressed home their attack with great determination.

Skipping through a wall of anti-aircraft fire two Italian bombers

Eugene Esmonde on *Ark Royal*.

headed directly for the *Ark Royal*, obviously intent on killing the carrier. The first bore in at the port side of the carrier until, as it filled their sight, the port multiple pom-pom battery opened fire, hitting the aircraft in the belly and detonating its torpedo. The wreckage fell all around in a hail of splintered metal. Its companion behind, flying in on the same course, began shedding metal as the pom-pom shells began to score hits on its fuselage and wings; then, less than 200 yards from its target, the bomber plunged nose-first into the sea. HMS *Nelson* received a torpedo hit, struggled on and, at nightfall, began a slow journey back to Gibraltar; while just one of the merchant ships, *Imperial Star*, was lost, the remaining eight reaching Grand Harbour, Valetta, just before noon on 28 September.

This pattern of convoy escorts and aircraft deliveries was to continue throughout October; often running a gauntlet of aerial and/or surface attacks, yet – perhaps astonishingly – the *Ark Royal* (generally dubbed the 'Bullshit Boat' by other, envious (?) RN personnel of Force H) continued to survive each attempted assault unscathed. She seemed to bear a charmed life – a 'lucky ship'_ On 13 November 1941 the *Ark*'s luck finally drained away. Days before the carrier had embarked twenty-four Hurricane IIs of No 242 Squadron RAF, plus a dozen more of No 605 Squadron RAF, between herself and the vintage carrier *Argus* – all to be delivered to Malta. These were duly flown off the carriers' decks on 12 November, then the *Ark* began its return journey to Gibraltar, accompanied by *Argus*, *Malaya*, *Hermione*, and seven destroyers.

Next day, 13 November, a Thursday, the weather was living up to full Mediterranean standards – warm, lazy sunshine, a calm sea, and crystal-blue skies. The *Ark Royal*'s crews off-duty were taking full benefit from it – a day for relaxing, for 'make-and-mend', letters home, or plain refurbishing a sun-tan. Enemy air attacks were unlikely, though gun crews were at their posts scanning the sky methodically in each direction, and radar screens were empty of unfamiliar blips. Less than a day's sail away lay the all-too familiar Rock of Gibraltar and the prospect of a day or two's shore leave once the ship had been replenished and prepared for its next voyage.

On the flight deck aircraft were being flown off and on; partly for further experience for the younger crews, and mainly as a daily routine of anti-submarine search and reconnaissance. In particular, Eugene Esmonde was ensuring that his air and 'ground' crews were kept busy – a constant ploy maintained throughout his tenure of command of 825 Squadron. At 3.25 pm, when the carrier was within thirty miles of Gibraltar and its towering Rock was already visible, twelve Swordfish took off in succession for a straightforward training exercise, while fourteen other aircraft, already airborne in the vicinity, patiently waited their turns to land back on. Just sixteen minutes later the ship shuddered under the impact of an explosion on its starboard flank, and the giant ship's electric power system immediately failed, dousing all lighting below decks and silencing the carrier's internal broadcasting network. The *Ark* staggered abruptly, jerking five aircraft awaiting lifts down to their hangars and bouncing them off the deck.

Hours earlier two German U-boats, *U-205* and *U-81*, had managed to elude the tight Allied defensive blockade across the Atlantic entrance to the Mediterranean. Once inside the Mediterranean the commander of *U-81*, Kapitänleutnant Guggenberger, received a signal, several hours old, instructing him to join forces with *U-205* in locating and attacking a British naval force thought to be approaching Gibraltar. By a combination of calculation, experience, and a modicum of sheer intelligent guesswork, Guggenberger worked out the most probable location of the enemy force and set course accordingly.

Shortly after 2 pm his calculations were proved correct; through his periscopic sights he spotted the mastheads of about a dozen warships on his horizon. He called his crew to action stations and cautiously closed the range; then, shortly after 3.30 pm, gave the orders to launch a salvo of four torpedoes in rapid succession. At least one torpedo found its mark on the aircraft carrier, while a second struck the *Malaya*.

The *Ark Royal*, which had been hit in the starboard boiler room, immediately took on a list of ten degrees, increasing to 12 degrees within three minutes, but continued to sail ahead at some 15 knots. By 4 pm the list to starboard had increased to some 18 degrees, while below decks serious flooding was adding to the danger of the carrier capsizing. Captain Maund issued orders for all nonessential personnel to leave the ship, and the destroyer *Legion* skilfully took up position on the *Ark*'s port quarter and began embarking the carrier's crew of some 1540 officers and men. Maund remained aboard his ship, along with certain key men, still hoping to keep the carrier afloat long enough to reach Gibraltar.

At 4.48 pm the *Legion* cast off from the *Ark*, and another destroyer, *Laforey*, came alongside to provide water and electrical power for the carrier's pumps. Slowly steam was raised in the *Ark*, the dynamos and steering engine came back into action, the *Laforey* cast off, and a chartered tug arrived about 7.30 pm. Taking the crippled carrier on tow, the tug managed to haul the ship forward at some two knots' speed, despite heading into a full knot current.

By somewhat tardy counter-flooding the carrier's frightening starboard list was eased to a less critical angle; then the Admiralty tug *St Day* appeared alongside and linked up to assist in the towing on the port side. Aboard the carrier Captain Maund and his skeleton 'crew' began to feel more confident that they might still reach Gibraltar, but at 2.15 am on 14 November a fire erupted in the port boiler room thereby nullifying all salvaging work for two hours. The ominous list increased to 20 degrees.

Once more the *Laforey* hove alongside, enabling a proportion of electrical power to be available for the *Ark*'s pumps and lighting but insufficient to fully restore enough power. The *Laforey* was next ordered forward to assist in the tug-work, thereby increasing forward speed to some five knots, but Gibraltar still lay twenty-five miles away. By 4 am the list had become 27 degrees, and by 4.30 am had increased to 35 degrees. Accepting defeat in his efforts Captain Maund gave the final order to abandon ship. Ropes were cast abreast of the tug *St Day* to the *Laforey* and the remaining 250 men aboard the *Ark* slid down these to safety, Maund being the last man to leave.

Once safely aboard *Laforey* Maund and his crew watched silently as their beloved *Ark Royal* continued slowly tilting on its side, the flight deck soon reaching a vertical stance. Then, at 6.13 am the carrier turned completely over, bottom upwards for a few minutes, then slid almost gracefully below the sea surface; its grave marker a huge, expanding ugly patch of dark oil on the water. With her in her final plunge to the depths was the body of Able Seaman E.

Ark Royal shortly after being torpedoed, 13 November 1941, with some of her Swordfish brood
stranded on the forward deck.

Ark Royal on 14 November 1941, with the destroyer *Laforey* alongside taking off the *Ark's* crew.

Mitchell – the sole fatal casualty, drowned while sleeping during the initial flooding caused by the torpedo's impact.

When the *Ark Royal* was hit by *U-81*'s torpedo, Eugene Esmonde's first concern, naturally, was for his squadron personnel and aircraft. Those Swordfish already airborne were instructed to fly to Gibraltar, but the aircraft aboard the carrier had no possibility of taking-off due to the sharp lilt of the flight deck within minutes of the torpedo strike. Esmonde therefore confined himself to ensuring his (and other) crews received all possible help in eventually reaching safety. Though offered the chance to leave the sinking carrier with the first, main evacuation of the ship's crew, Esmonde insisted on remaining aboard as one of Maund's 'skeleton crew', and appointed himself temporary catering officer by arranging the ready supply of food and refreshments for the remaining personnel as these toiled to save the ship. As such he was the only pilot left aboard during the final hours of the *Ark*'s life. When eventually leaving the ship with the last survivors, Esmonde continued to see to the welfare of his men, including their spiritual needs in the case of fellow Roman Catholics by arranging for a local priest at Gibraltar to attend them.*

Once ashore at Gibraltar Esmonde was faced with yet another reconstruction programme for his 825 Squadron. In the event he received instructions to transfer a few men to local FAA units, but the bulk of the crews were embarked in HMS *Nelson* and sailed to England, where they reassembled at Lee-on-Solent, still designated 825 Squadron under Esmonde's command, but having to almost completely re-equip with fresh Swordfish aircraft and the myriad ancillary equipment needed by a potential operational squadron. For his part in the final drama of the *Ark Royal* Eugene Esmonde was 'Mentioned in Despatches', not simply for the final hours of that poignant affair but – as the *London Gazette* citation dated 20 January 1942 described – 'For courage, enterprise and resolution in air attacks on the enemy'.

* The *Ark Royal*'s chaplain then was the late Noel Chamberlain, later Chaplain of the Fleet who retired as a Bishop, who was Church of England faith.

CHAPTER EIGHT

Prelude

On his return to Lee-on-Solent from Gibraltar, Eugene Esmonde began the now familiar process of rebuilding 825 Squadron to an operationally ready status. Fortunately on this occasion many of the existing crews of the squadron remained under his command, while the few 'losses', i.e. men transferred to other FAA units, were soon to be replaced by fresh air crews, mainly from FAA training schools and therefore new to the operational scene. The supply of replacement aircraft, again Fairey Swordfish torpedo-bombers, was slightly tardy despite there being a relatively large quantity of the type in FAA service then.

By that time Esmonde had been in command of 825 Squadron for some eighteen months, an unusually lengthy period in such an appointment. Moreover, virtually the whole of his command had been on firstline operational activities; a period of continuous active duty which, had Esmonde occupied a similar post on an RAF squadron, might have normally led to his posting to some non-operational appointment for a rest spell. Apart from Esmonde's personal wish to remain in command of 825 Squadron, it is quite probable that the FAA's lack of sufficient pilots with Esmonde's rank and experience by late 1941 had some bearing on his continuance in his post.

Having set in motion all necessary administrative channels for fresh crews, aircraft and equipment for 825 Squadron's latest rebirth at Lee-on-Solent, and whilst awaiting a decision from the Admiralty as to his unit's future employment, Eugene Esmonde took some leave, returning to Drominagh for the Christmas and early New Year holidays. Here he spent much of his time simply enjoying the peace and quiet of familiar surroundings, and in the company of Antonia, wife of his elder brother Owen, and her (then) two daughters Deborah Ann and Gillian, both very young babies;* their father, Owen, being on duty as a Pilot Officer, RAF with a barrage balloon unit at Sheffield, England.

Though obviously genuinely happy when playing with the children in the grounds of the family home, Esmonde in other moments seemed to Antonia to be more than usually quiet, even withdrawn, and rather depressed. One evening he mentioned to her that he was soon to be taken off combat flying and would be given an instructional post in a few months' time; a prospect to which he was not particularly looking forward. Whether in fact any such future appointment had actually been mentioned to him by higher authority at that time is at least questionable, and this statement may have been simply a kindly ploy on Esmonde's part to allay any anxiety felt by his mother and relatives for his future safety.

Various past published accounts of Eugene Esmonde have inferred that he was at that period convinced of his imminent fate, a fey knowledge of his death in the very near future. There is no concrete recorded evidence of any such apprehension as far as can be ascertained, though such an abstract thought cannot be entirely dismissed. If indeed Eugene Esmonde felt any such precognisance, it was not overtly obvious to those whom he met during that Christmas leave period. Certainly, Esmonde appeared to be reflective, even on occasion reminiscent of his earlier years, whilst at Drominagh. Looking out over a large field behind the grey house, he remembered the time during his RAF service when he had been granted a 48-hours' leave and decided to spend his journey home by flying the last leg of his travel. Borrowing a small biplane owned by a cousin Osmonde Esmonde, a member of the Dail Eirran, Eugene had picked up his youngest brother, Patrick, from Dublin and landed in that field – the first time an aeroplane had ever landed in the district and therefore creating great excitement locally.

Eugene had then taken Owen for his first-ever flight, including a full loop above the shimmering waters of Lough Derg, and later

---

* Of a further four children born to Antonia and Owen Esmonde, their first son, Eugene born in August 1942, was named in memory of his late uncle.

gave a local friend, Dennis Fogarty his first sight of his neighbourhood from the air. Next day Eugene flew the tiny biplane on a brief round visit to several relatives in the area. Those carefree times now seemed so far away to Eugene ...

During that last leave Eugene visited his half-brother Tony (now Sir Anthony Esmonde, Bt) and, despite it being several years since he had ridden a horse, took part in the traditional Christmas hunt – and suffered several unseatings in the process. During later conversation Eugene mentioned to Anthony that when the *Ark Royal* was finally abandoned prior to its sinking he had been the last to leave, excepting the Captain, and that his last duty aboard the carrier had been to go below decks searching through the eerie unlit compartments for the ship's secret papers, then carrying these in their lead-weighted container bag to safety.

Asked by Anthony if he was ever afraid when flying on operations, Eugene replied that he was always 'afraid of *being* afraid' – an indication, perhaps, of his innermost conviction that as a leader and commander of men in action he had to at least appear fully calm and confident by personal example. Eugene also remarked that after all his recent experiences he treasured the moment when, while passing through Dublin on his way to home, he had paused on the O'Connell Bridge and revelled in the myriad lights and the peace of the city – such a vivid contrast to the wartime Britain he had so recently left behind him.

As Eugene's leave came to an end, his thoughts reverted to the task awaiting him at Lee-on-Solent, that of building up 825 Squadron to operational strength and fitness. By early January 1942, despite all his efforts, the squadron still only comprised six Swordfish aircraft and six complete three-man crews, plus a seventh pilot. Yet at Lee-on-Solent then were at least twenty-four other Swordfish and a fair number of air crew men. Admittedly most of the latter were 'green' in the context of operational training or experience, but Esmonde's tiny band of air crews were hardly better trained. All six of the rating TAGs had seen previous active flying service, including A.L. 'Ginger' Johnson DSM from the *Bismarck* affair.

Of the pilots and Observers only two pilots and four Observers had any operational experience under their belts. One of these

Observers, for example, was Edgar Lee, who had joined 825
Squadron by May 1941 and served under Esmonde aboard the *Ark
Royal*. Another Observer, Reginald McCartney Samples – 'Mac' –
was only too typical of about half of Esmonde's crews. Trained as a
Naval Observer on No 45 Observers Course in Trinidad, 'Mac' had
only just returned to England when he received his orders to join
825 Squadron at Lee-on-Solent – his first operational posting. The
orders barely gave him time to procure a uniform before his joining
date. Equally green in experience was Charles Kingsmill, a Sub-
Lieutenant of twenty-one years, educated at Dulwich College, but
who had left his civilian desk-job to join the war, and had yet to
undertake an operational sortie.

Unbeknown to Eugene Esmonde at that time, he and his half-
strength, virtually untrained 'squadron' were about to become
involved in a long-running contingency plan of operations, *Operation
Fuller*. The background to *Fuller* essentially began on 28 March
1941, when Pilot Officer Green of the RAF's Photo Reconnaissance
Unit (PRU) flew over Brest harbour and his film revealed the
presence of the German battleships *Scharnhorst* and *Gneisenau*. These
deep-sea raiders had last been photographed on 21 December 1940
in Kiel, but a further PRU sortie over Kiel on 9 January 1941 had
shown empty berths – both battleships had indeed sailed from Kiel
on 27 December and eventually broken into the open Atlantic,
where over the following three months they had preyed on Allied
shipping, sinking some 115,000 tons between them, before putting
into Brest on 22 March 1941, here to receive necessary refitting.

The presence of *Scharnhorst* and *Gneisenau* at Brest posed a serious
problem for the British Admiralty immediately. At the end of
March 1941 the Admiralty's two main operational priorities were,
first, the trans-Atlantic merchant shipping convoys bringing
crucially vital war materials to Britain to sustain the UK's war
effort, and, second, was the British Home Fleet's commitment to
protect a series of very large troop convoys from Britain to the
Middle East in order to reinforce the British Eighth Army *et al* then
engaged in a desperate struggle along the northern coast territories
of North Africa.

The battleships at Brest now presented an open threat to both of
those priorities, but these merely added to the Admiralty's existing

(Right) Sub-Lieutenant Edgar Lee on *Ark Royal*, 25 October 1941.

(Below) Personnel of 31 SFTS, Kingston, Ontario, commanded by Commander G.N.P. Stringer (seated 2nd from left). Seated far right is Sub-Lieutenant Edgar Lee, DSO, one of the survivors of the 'Channel Dash' action. Photo taken 1942.

G.I.S. BUILDING

worries about other German naval raiders which might pose equal
threats to Allied shipping in the Atlantic; in particular the *Bismarck*,
Prinze Eugen, Admiral Scheer, apart from the *Tirpitz* which Allied
intelligence indicated would be ready for operations soon. All these
were stationed in northern waters at that time, necessitating the
British to retain much of their Home Fleet at Scapa Flow, ready to
intercept any moves by German battleships into the open Atlantic
via the Denmark Straits gateway.

Thus this splitting of Germany's greatest naval threats
geographically had the effect of holding the British Home Fleet in a
cleft stick at the beginning of April 1941; a dilemma urgently discussed and analysed at a series of Admiralty and RAF hierarchy
meetings during that month. Of the two Services the Royal Navy
was clearly the most hampered in the context of positive offensive
remedial action to such a situation. Its myriad commitments to
protection of convoys in the Atlantic, Mediterranean, and other
vital sea lanes, added to its necessary watchdog role in the North
Sea was already stretching its overall capacity to the limits. Accordingly, it was agreed in principle that only the RAF might be able
to nullify the threat of the Brest-based battleships, and RAF
Bomber Command was therefore called upon to divert a reasonable
proportion of its contemporary offensive strength to attacks on the
Atlantic seaboard ports of France. It would mean diluting an
already relatively weak offensive by the bombers against Germany,
but the naval situation was, for the moment, considered to be the
higher priority.

Taking in all hypothetical and practical facets of that situation, a
directive from the Air Ministry to RAF Bomber, Fighter, and
Coastal Commands, dated 29 April 1941, outlined the various
possible future moves by the German battleships, then offered their
counter-moves to be actioned by the RAF commands. Clause 7 of
this directive – which had been given the code-name *Operation Fuller*
– is of particular interest in the hindsight of later events:

> It is considered unlikely that the enemy would attempt the
> passage of the (Dover) Straits in daylight. If however this should
> be attempted a unique opportunity will be offered to both our
> surface vessels and air striking forces to engage the enemy ships

in force whilst in the Straits of Dover. Such attacks are to be delivered to the *maximum practicable effort under fighter cover* [Author's italics] to be provided by the Air Officer Commanding-in-Chief Fighter Command. The Admiralty are arranging that in these circumstances the VA Dover (Vice-Admiral Bertram W. Ramsay) will keep 11 Group (Fighter Command) and 16 Group (Coastal Command) informed of attacks carried out by surface vessels in order that air attacks may be co-ordinated therewith and fighter cover provided.

The AOC-in-Cs of RAF Fighter and Coastal Commands in 1941 were, respectively, Air Marshal Sholto Douglas and Air Chief Marshal Sir Philip Joubert, while the Air Officer Commanding (AOC) of Fighter Command's No 11 Group was Air Vice-Marshal Trafford Leigh-Mallory, responsible for all fighter operations in south-eastern England. For Bomber Command's part in *Fuller*, its AOC-in-C, Air Marshal Sir Richard Peirse said in his directive dated 1 May: 'If the passage of the ships is attempted they will be attacked by surface craft and aircraft *by day*. It is not intended that aircraft should attack by night.'

With the advantage of postwar research evidence, it is of no little interest to realise that when the initial directive for *Operation Fuller* was issued from the Air Ministry, no plans for any such 'Channel Dash' operation had even been suggested among the German higher commands. The strategic effect of having the 'Ugly Sisters' – as *Scharnhorst* and *Gneisenau* were lightly dubbed by the RAF bomber crews – stationed at Brest appeared so obvious to the German naval commanders that any suggestion of transferring them to Baltic ports simply had not arisen. The loss of the *Bismarck* on 27 May, however, changed the whole German naval outlook in the context of future operations in the Atlantic. It was apparent that the passage route to the Atlantic via the Denmark Straits would no longer be viable, and some other route had to be considered for any capital ships harboured in Norway and the Baltic. Such an alternative was first suggested on 30 May 1941 by the German naval command in France to Berlin – to use the English Channel *from east to west*. After careful consideration of this novel idea, the Berlin Naval War Staff gave as its opinion; ' ... an unobserved and safe escape (*sic*) through the Channel would be impossible'.

In view of this pragmatic pronouncement by those most concerned in any such venture, it remains somewhat puzzling that the British Admiralty and Air Ministry should have even considered such a possibility of the Germans actually removing *Scharnhorst* and *Gneisenau* from Brest, or at least some other French port nearby. While remaining there they were a 'grey eminence' on the Atlantic and even Mediterranean naval scene; a Damocles' sword hanging over all Allied naval intentions. The only reasonable answer would seem to be a contemporary over-optimistic reliance on the destructive power of the RAF 'heavy' bombers if these were unleashed on a series of attacks on Brest and La Pallice, the principal German naval ports along the western French coastline.

Bomber Command's diversion of effort against Brest and other likely harbours for the German battleships in the latter months of 1941 was pressed home on all occasions with great determination and courage, but with no small casualty rates and in virtual 'penny-packet' strengths. The only 'heavy' bombers with sufficient range to reach such targets then available to Bomber Command were Short Stirlings, Handley Page Halifaxes, and a handful of Boeing B-17 Fortress Is – the latter equipping merely one unit, No 90 Squadron RAF. Since almost all such raids were flown in daylight the bombers were highly vulnerable to both anti-aircraft (*flak*) fire and Luftwaffe fighter opposition; while few such sorties could be protected by RAF fighter escorts, there being few RAF fighters then capable of flying and operating at such combat ranges. Even had the bomber formations despatched emerged unscathed – a rare occurrence – their gross weight and types of bombs dropped over the target were insufficient to have any permanent effect on armoured-deck battleships. On the other hand, direct or even near-miss bombs could and did cause some damage and casualties to the ships, thereby keeping the battleships in need of repairs and replacements in personnel – in itself a method of preventing the ships leaving harbour to undertake oceanic operations. The need for a constant watch on the enemy ports, was exemplified on 1 June 1941 when a third naval raider, *Prinz Eugen*, put into Brest on return from the *Bismarck* episode – an 'arrival' confirmed three days later by RAF reconnaissance film.

Throughout the rest of 1941 and early 1942 *Operation Fuller* remained in force, albeit in the light of a steady stream of secret intelligence supplied by various Allied agents and Frenchmen sympathetic to the Allied cause of the damages caused by the many RAF bombing forays the urgency of *Fuller* had begun to fade by the year's end. Nevertheless, occasional new orders were issued internally within RAF commands from time to time, re-emphasising each command's individual intentions. Despite such orders, however, the strictest level of 'security' was imposed from the beginning on the purpose of *Fuller*; this being known only to the most senior officers in each RAF command and a relative handful of very senior RN officers. Only they were aware of the command *Executive Fuller* which, theoretically, would unleash the combined air and naval forces in the planned sequence of actions designed to destroy any German naval force in the English Channel. This ultra-secrecy was to be maintained until the very day that the German battleships threaded their way through the Dover Straits – a cloak of 'security' which was to have tragic results in the final reckoning of the events of 12 February 1942.

The idea of bringing *Scharnhorst*, *Gneisenau*, and *Prinz Eugen* from Brest to German ports via the English Channel came from the German Führer, Adolf Hitler. On 17 September 1941 Admiral Erich Raeder, commander-in-chief of the German navy, attended a conference at Hitler's 'Wolf's Lair' residence, where he was told by Hitler that all German battleships would be better employed guarding Norway from an anticipated (by Hitler only ...) Allied invasion of that country. Though placated by Raeder's arguments against any such redeployment at that moment, Hitler reintroduced the subject at a November conference, being even more convinced by his 'intuition' by then that the Allies would invade Norway.

Eventually, in December, Hitler issued an ultimatum to his naval chiefs – either move all three battleships from Brest or he would have them dismantled and their heavy guns sent to join the defences of Norway. In the face of such imperious orders Raeder had no choice but to set in motion plans for the ships' evacuation from Brest to Germany (initially) with an eventual venue in

Norwegian ports. Hitler's decision had been based mainly on two items – his 'intuitive' conviction of an invasion of Norway by Allied forces, and, though secondary, a blunt assurance by Hermann Göring, Luftwaffe supremo, that the Luftwaffe was simply not strong enough to provide an adequate permanent aerial defence of Brest due to the increasing commitments of the air arm in Russia, North Africa, and in defence of the Reich from Allied bombers.

Actual planning for the Channel venture began on 12 January 1942 under the personal aegis of Admiral Otto Ciliax, overall commander of the Brest Group, a graduate of the Flensburg Naval Academy whose draconian views on discipline and general unpopularity with his subordinates had led to his soubriquet of 'The Black Czar'. Ciliax had, initially, been opposed to Hitler's scheme, but on later reflection had decided in favour of the basic idea of a quick dash over such a short route, rather than invite the myriad hazards of any alternative journey of much longer duration e.g. around north of Britain.

Accordingly, Ciliax had a meticulously detailed and comprehensive plan drawn up under the code-name *Cerebus** with no facet of same permitting ambiguity or individual 'interpretation'. His covering order made it quite plain to all concerned that no deviation from the plan in *any* detail was to be countenanced – only 100 per cent adherence would ensure success *if* such was attainable. As with the British counter-plan *Fuller*, total security blanketing was vital in the preliminary preparation; hence full knowledge of the escape plan was known only to Ciliax, his chief of staff, Kapitän H.J. Reinicke, the three battleship captains, Kurt Hoffman (*Scharnhorst*), Otto Fein (*Gneisenau*), and Helmuth Brinkmann (*Prinz Eugen*), the senior destroyer commander, and a handful of specific naval staff officers. One other person necessarily 'in the picture' had to be Helmuth Giessler, navigator on the *Scharnhorst*, the ship in which Ciliax intended to hoist his flag and actually lead the trio of battleships on *Cerebus*.

The timing of the actual voyage at each stage was crucial.

---

* In the initial stages, for secrecy reasons, five different code names were used, and *Cerebus* was not used until the final commitment to proceed was decided. The air cover plan by the Luftwaffe was separately coded *Thunderbolt*.

Ideally, the aim was to sail from Brest in the early evening darkness of a no-moon night – in early February such a night would provide some twelve hours' darkness from 7.30 pm to about 7.30 am until 15 February which would be a full moon – and preferably in weather conditions of low cloud and reduced visibility. Since the most favourable tides and currents would occur between 7 and 15 February, and the German meteorological observers forecast such 'favourable weather' for 11 February; the actual sailing date was decided to be in the evening of that date, with zero hour fixed at 7.30 pm. If all went according to plan such a sailing time should ensure the naval force entering the Dover Straits at about mid-day on 12 February – by which time some two-thirds of the voyage would be behind it.

The essence of the whole *Cerebus* plan was surprise – to stalk in darkness up the French coast and along the length of the English Channel, hopefully to be undetected until daylight by which time the force would be leaving the gauntlet area between the English and French coastlines. Had it left Brest by day, the chances of discovery by the RAF and/or Royal Navy at the western Channel approach area would have been greatly enhanced, and the subsequent dash through the narrow Channel would have been scoured continuously by well-alerted defences all along the route to Dover.

Viewed objectively, the choice between sailing the length of the Channel by day or by night could only lay with the latter option – such was Hitler's and therefore Ciliax's decision. That the British Services' hierarchy should have thought that the *former* option would be the most probable course of action taken by any German escape attempt remains near-incredible, even allowing for hindsight. Certainly, mention had been made in *Fuller* of both options, yet the prime emphasis of that contingency plan relied upon the conviction of a *daylight* run from Cornwall to the open North Sea.

The surface and air umbrella for the trio of battleships was relatively formidable. Planned to increase by stages along the intended route, the initial escort out of Brest and up to the eastward turn round Cherbourg comprised seven destroyers flanking the main ships (though in the event one destroyer was sunk by a mine), after which they would be joined successively by a total of fifteen torpedo-boats; while the way ahead would be 'flushed' of Allied seamines by a force of German mine-sweepers. The ports at Cherbourg, Le Havre, Flushing, and Hook of Holland were prepared in advance as possible refuges should such bolt-holes become necessary. For aerial protection the famed fighter virtuoso Adolf Galland was summoned to Hitler's 'Wolf's Lair' and personally ordered by the German Führer to provide the strongest possible continuous air cover to the seaborne formation.

After discussion with Ciliax aboard *Scharnhorst* Galland quickly prepared a complex air defence organisation. With his personal command post located at Le Touquet, roughly the halfway point of the route, and subsidiary posts at Caen and Schiphol for the early and late legs respectively, Galland could muster a gross total of 282 fighter aircraft for '*Thunderbolt*'. This total was comprised of 252 Messerschmitt Bf 109Fs and Focke Wulf Fw 190As from *Jagdgeschwader* (JG) 1, 2, 26, and training units at Abbeville, plus 30 Junkers Ju 88 and Messerschmitt Bf 110 twin-engined nightfighters from *Nachtjagdgeschwader* 2 and 3.

As his central controller and liaison officer with the naval force Galland selected Oberst Max Ibel, a veteran fighter *Experte* ('ace') and placed him aboard *Scharnhorst*. By carefully timed overlapping of airborne escort patrols, Galland arranged for a minimum force of sixteen fighters to be over the ships at all times, slotting into periods of changeover which would provide up to thirty-two fighters at each end of these patrols. Refuelling and re-arming of each patrol was to be accomplished progressively along a string of Luftwaffe airfields in France and Holland as the seaborne formation moved eastwards along the Channel. In the event of any standing patrol being attacked by the RAF it would be swiftly reinforced by all combat-ready Luftwaffe fighters within fighting range.

The aerial facets of the British contingency counter-plan, *Fuller*, appeared – at least, on paper – to have been prepared for most alternatives of any intended break-out from Brest of the German battleships. Apart from the normal day and night air patrols over the Bay of Biscay and the western coastal zones of France mounted regularly by RAF Coastal Command, individual aircraft fitted with Air to Surface Vessel (ASV) radar sets were despatched regularly to cover three designated patrol lines; *Stopper* (off the entrance to Brest itself), *Line SE* (from Ushant to Ile de Brehat), and *Habo* (Le Havre to Boulogne). In addition, Fighter Command's No 11 Group despatched *Jim Crow* patrols, usually pairs of Spitfires, to fly general reconnaissances of the Channel area, and despatched every two hours from dawn to dusk.

In support, and theoretically in operational readiness state, were three squadrons of Bristol Beaufort torpedo-bombers, Nos 42, 86, and 217. These in turn were to be escorted by fighters from No 11 Group, while Bomber Command, which had spent the first weeks of February 1942 laying mines athwart any probable sea route, was expected to back up all other forces with medium and heavy bombers when called upon. The general opinion among Admiralty and RAF senior officers was that the prime attacking weapon would be the torpedo-bombers which, if not actually sinking any of the enemy battleships, might at least cripple them and leave them at a disadvantage in manoeuvring when Royal Navy surface and RAF air forces attacked later. Obviously, those officers had in mind the recent *Bismarck* affair and the huge success achieved by a handful of FAA Swordfish against the Italian Fleet at Taranto.

One other air unit to become included in the *Fuller* plan was Eugene Esmonde's 825 Squadron. The decision to include a 'force' (*sic*) of Swordfish came from Vice-Admiral Ramsay at Dover, who shared a majority opinion among the *Fuller* planners that the German ships would pass through the Dover Straits *in darkness*, probably some two hours before dawn, and could therefore be relatively safely attacked by the vintage Swordfish in the protective cloak of night, without need for fighter escort. Accordingly, an order went to Esmonde to transfer his squadron from Lee-on-Solent to the RAF forward airfield at Manston, Kent.

Only days before receipt of this order, Esmonde had been one of a number of squadron commanders present at a secret conference attended by several very senior Admiralty and Air Ministry officers where the basics of *Operation Fuller* were revealed to the fliers. It was made plain to Esmonde and his fellow unit commanders that their part would be a combined effort of FAA and RAF torpedo bombers, in conjunction with other army and naval forces, and would be made *by night*. It was also indicated that, as far as the FAA element was concerned, participation would be on a voluntary basis. In the light of the circumstances as explained at this conference, Esmonde quietly volunteered his squadron. On 4 February 1942 he flew at the head of his six Swordfish through a snow blizzard to Manston, being joined there next day by the ground maintenance staff under the command of Edgar Lee who had travelled by road.

On arrival at Manston Eugene reported to the RAF commander of the station, Wing Commander Tom Gleave, an ex-Battle of Britain veteran fighter pilot, but made no mention of the true reason for the presence of his unit beyond a slightly vague reference to his need to instigate an intensive training programme for his mainly raw air crews in the technique of low-level torpedo strikes. Gleave was already aware of the *Fuller* plan itself, but had not yet been given any hint on the imminence of the actual break-out from Brest. As Gleave commented later*, 'Esmonde was meticulous in his attitude to security. It would have helped me greatly to know that the Ugly Sisters were ready to make a dash for it any day (at that time), but Esmonde kept mute about it despite our closest co-operation in all other matters. He was not to blame. The degree of secrecy surrounding the steps to be taken in the event of a break-out by the Ugly Sisters was the cause – it was unbelievable.'

Gleave also gave his personal impression of Eugene as 'A small, dapper little fellow. Alert and intelligent, he was a pleasant conversationalist with a touch of that individualism which Steve† had possessed to such a marked degree. It was easy to like Esmonde … he took his duties seriously, and although I never interfered with nor indeed enquired about the management of No 825 Squadron FAA, it was abundantly clear to me that Esmonde was an efficient CO for whom those under him had a great respect.'

As with all other air squadrons earmarked for *Operation Fuller* Esmonde's 825 began a daily routine of coming to full readiness state at 4 am each morning, only to be stood down at dawn – an indication of the Admiralty's adherence to the conviction still that

---

* Letter to the author, 1971.

† Referring to Squadron Leader R.P. Stevens, DSO, DFC, a famed Hurricane nightfighter pilot, killed in action 15 December 1941.

the enemy ships would breach the Channel by night – after which 825's crews continued the training programme instituted by Esmonde; a programme which, in Esmonde's personal opinion, would necessitate at least four weeks' duration if his crews were to be fully efficient to normal operational standards. Meanwhile he attempted to obtain more crews and aircraft to bring his squadron up to full fighting strength. At Lee-on-Solent alone were dozens of Swordfish aircraft, to his personal knowledge, yet his official entreaties were met with bland statements that no experienced crews were available to man these – a 'reason' which smacked of pure irony considering the half-trained status of half of 825 Squadron's existing air crews.

Meantime Esmonde kept his few crews on constant day and night practice for their intended role. His initial ideas for any actual attack was to approach the ships from their front, splitting the force into two sub-Flights once within torpedo range and attacking from both port and starboard quarters simultaneously in order to minimise the effect of anti-aircraft gunfire, yet at the same time to maximise confusion among the enemy gunners as to which targets to engage. In order to get his crews to the most efficient state of crew co-operation, Esmonde detailed each crew by name, leaving only the question of which of his seven pilots would actually man each aircraft. This decision was settled simply – the two most junior pilots, Sub-Lieutenants Peter Bligh and Bennett tossed a coin. Bligh called 'Tails' and won, thus young Bennett was to remain on the ground at Manston unless some unforeseen circumstance caused any of the other six pilots to become incapacitated. Esmonde's second-in-command was to be Lieutenant J.C. Thompson, a regular-serving RN officer-pilot.

In the event of being brought into action by night – as was expected under the terms of *Fuller* – 825 Squadron was to be 'controlled' from the RAF station at Swingate, Dover; while ahead of the Swordfish would fly Hurricanes from Manston whose job would be to drop illuminating flares over the enemy ships and thereby offer the Swordfish crews a clear sight of their objectives. These Hurricanes would be supplied by one or more of the resident units based at Manston then, Nos 607 and 615 Squadrons, and the night intruders of No 3 Squadron. Out on Manston's snow-encrusted grass airfield 825 Squadron's Swordfish were parked in the open dispersal adjacent to 607 Squadron's Hurricane IIBs, and the ground crews of both units often 'mucked in' to help each other, despite the traditional friendly rivalry between 'Fish-heads' and 'Brylcreem Boys' – the universal lightly insulting nicknames for RN and RAF personnel respectively used by airmen and seamen of the period. Off duty 825's non-commissioned ratings shared the RAF Sergeants' Mess accommodation, an evacuated children's nursing home in Westgate.

On Wednesday, 11 February, Eugene Esmonde left Manston and drove to Margate to catch a train to London, there to attend an investiture ceremony at Buckingham Palace to receive the Distinguished Service Order (DSO) he had been awarded for his part in the hunting of the *Bismarck* a year before. He intended to visit the Admiralty before going to the Palace, in the hope of obtaining more aircraft and crews *et al* for his squadron, but his train was an hour late arriving in London, leaving him little time to book into a hotel, change into full dress uniform and proceed to the Palace. Here he met his former Observer, Colin Ennever, also due to be decorated, and spent a pleasant hour reminiscing of their time aboard the *Ark Royal* and the *Victorious*. Once the ceremony was over, the two attended a dinner given by Admiral Somerville, but once this duty was completed Esmonde declined politely to join Ennever on any further celebration and made his way back to Manston by the next available train.

Even as Eugene Esmonde was preparing to attend Admiral Somerville's celebratory dinner in his (and others') honour, events were taking place hundreds of miles away in Brest harbour which were to prove fateful. Earlier that evening Admiral Ciliax had issued an order to all vessels under his West Group command; 'Prepare to proceed on exercise' – an apparent directive to undertake night training manoeuvres between La Pallice and St Nazaire, with a return to harbour in Brest in the evening of 12 February. In fact, this was a final attempt to allay any suspicions as to the actual intention – the break-out.

Operation Cerebus was about to commence, albeit without the knowledge of all but the very few senior officers already in the secret, and actual sailing time was set for 7.30 pm. At precisely that

Head-on view of *Scharnhorst* on 12 February 1942, showing the many additional flak guns supplementing the ship's main guns.

hour the *Scharnhorst*'s crew began slipping their mooring ropes, and the ship's signallers were about to flash sailing orders to the rest of the ships, when Brest's air raid sirens began their howling dirge – the RAF were expected at any moment. Within minutes the first bombs began falling onto Brest as seventeen Wellingtons from No 1 Group, RAF Bomber Command began their attack. Across the harbour dense clouds of artificial fog began to envelope the waiting ships as the harbour defences sprang into action.

For the next forty-five minutes the raid continued until the last Wellington had released its bomb load, during which period one raider from No 150 Squadron was shot down. Some bombs found their marks in the town itself, but none hit any of the waiting ships. Though the raid ceased by 8.30 pm, the 'all-clear' sirens were not sounded until 9.14 pm. Ciliax's orders had included the proviso that any delay in sailing of more than two hours after 7.30 pm would involve postponement of *Cerebus* – accordingly he gave the order to sail immediately. Given good fortune the ships could still make up the lost time and still break through the Channel at the precisely planned time.

With the flagship *Scharnhorst* in the lead, followed successively by *Gneisenau* and *Prinz Eugen*, the naval force inched out of Brest harbour and set a course due west initially to maintain the fiction of an 'exercise', then turned to starboard on their real course of 340 – a change which astonished the *Scharnhorst*'s officer of the watch, Wilhelm Wolf, who had yet to be told of the true nature of this 'exercise'. On querying the change of course to Helmuth Giessler, he received the cheerful reply, 'Course correct', then with a grin Giessler added, 'Tomorrow you'll be kissing your wife in Germany'.

The night above them was clear and starlit, the sea lightly swelling and with little wind, as the ships ploughed at maximum speed through a thin haze. By midnight they were sailing past Ushant, just seventy-two minutes behind schedule, and at the point of no return. At that point Admiral Ciliax addressed his crew aboard *Scharnhorst*, informing them for the first time of their imminent task – to sail through the Channel eastwards into the German Bight. *Operation Cerebus* was finally committed.

CHAPTER NINE

Running The Gauntlet

At 1615 hours on 11 February 1942 a lone, unarmed Spitfire piloted by Squadron Leader A.H.W. – 'Freddie' – Ball of the PRU detachment based at St Eval, Cornwall commenced his photographic runs across Brest filming the harbour below. On his return his film indicated that the three German battleships were tied up alongside refuelling wharves, with a number of attendant destroyers and other vessels nearby. This sortie was the last of 729 PRU photographic flights over the 'Ugly Sisters' in the preceding eleven months, during which period nine PRU aircraft had failed to return.

Freddie Ball's photographs seemed to prove that the trio of enemy ships were about to leave harbour, but an RAF bombing raid some three hours later returned with photographs showing the ships still in harbour. Accordingly, no report was sent to Coastal Command HQ, and no alarm was raised. It was the first of a succession of sheer mishaps and crucial errors to be made by the RAF and Royal Navy in the following hours. The three Coastal Command patrol lines of *Stopper*, *Line SE*, and *Habo* theoretically overlapped in areas and timing, thereby ostensibly ensuring that if one patrolling aircraft 'missed' the ships in its area, they were bound to be discovered by the adjacent patrol.

Throughout the night of 11/12 February, however, the Lockheed Hudsons from 224 Squadron (St Eval) and 223 Squadron (Thorney Island) flying their respective patrol lines suffered a series of radar and other technical faults, resulting in early returns to bases for rectification. The outcome was a coincidental 'chain' of gaps in each patrol area observation which permitted the German naval formation to sail through each area completely undetected from the air.

Nor were these unfortunate coincidences confined to the RAF.

Two RN submarines, HMS *Sealion* and *H.34*, had been stationed off Brest for many days and nights, awaiting any opportunity to attack any of the three battleships should these leave Brest for exercises. Each day at dawn *Sealion* moved in close to Brest, ready for action, but had to withdraw at dusk to recharge batteries. Since the enemy ships were not expected to sail by night, this 'guard' routine seemed logical. But on the night of 11 February when *Cerebus* got under way, *Sealion* was far west of any possible attacking location ... The irony here, though unbeknown to *Sealion*'s commander, was that had *Cerebus* sailed at 7.30 pm – its intended start time – the submarine was then still in an ideal position for attack just outside Brest harbour. The RAF's bombing raid which delayed departure also covered the time when *Sealion* was forced to withdraw to recharge batteries.

The sorry saga of missed opportunities, misinterpretation, and – to no small degree – sheer inefficiency and disorganisation of the British defences was now beginning to escalate. First of these misfortunes was the failure of various British radar stations along the southern coastline of England to identify the various German sea and air movements for what they were. In this context most of the radar operators could hardly be blamed. For some weeks prior to 11/12 February a system of gently increasing jamming of the various British radar signals had been under way, usually in short bursts which bore all the earmarks of atmospheric interference to the men and women watching radar screens in England. The build-up of this systematic jamming was carefully controlled not to excite suspicion, and by mid-February had become virtually accepted by British operators.

Such blips as did appear on British screens on 12 February were at first interpreted as fairly routine – German coastal shipping movements, Luftwaffe air-sea rescue patrols, air-testing of German aircraft stationed along the French coast – all familiar signals which need cause no alarm. The mistaken identification and interpretation of British radar plots was to continue for several hours during the early morning of Thursday, 12 February – 'lost' hours during which no positive action under the *Fuller* plan was initiated, and which were to be crucial in allowing the German battleships to escape almost certain destruction.

Apart from the various routine Coastal Command air patrols off the French coast, RAF Fighter Command – in this context, No 11 Group – also mounted daily routine air reconnaissance patrols by single or pairs of fighters across the Channel; sorties coded *Jim Crow* by the RAF. At 0845 hrs two Spitfires of No 91 Squadron left Hawkinge airfield for the day's first *Jim Crow* patrols, one of these heading northwards to Zeebrugge where its pilot noted an enemy merchant ship convoy; while his 'partner' flew to Cap Gris Nez and spotted a formation of German E-boats sailing southwards. Neither pilot reported their finds over their radios due to the existing Group order for strict R/T silence while airborne, and on return to base their findings were noted with mild interest. Neither pilot had ever heard of *Operation Fuller*, and were equally innocent of the expected breakout of the German ships from Brest; to them it had been merely one more slightly boring duty to enter up in their log books.

One hour before this pair of Spitfires had taken off the first sixteen Luftwaffe nightfighter escorts had rendezvoused with the naval formation, a little over one hour before dawn. They appeared on the British radar set at Beachy Head, but since the blips were not approaching England they were merely noted in the log, then ignored. At the time this first section of Adolf Galland's aerial escort met their charges, the German sea formation was fast approaching the Dieppe-Le Havre area, almost back on its original timing plan despite the two-hours' delay in starting out from Brest; in effect, well over the halfway stage of running the Channel gauntlet, and, as yet, undiscovered and unchallenged. Dawn that morning came shortly after 8 am in the Channel, a chilly dawn with mist, rain and low clouds, and as daylight flooded in slowly the leading ships were nearing the coast off Barfleur. Soon shafts of a wintry sun began penetrating the cloud ceiling and Admiral Ciliax and his many crews, still almost unbelieving of their luck at meeting no resistance as yet, now began anxiously to scour the sea and air for signs of the British 'Tommies' – surely, they *must* attack soon? They were, in fact, to enjoy another three hours of freedom from positive identification, and a further hour and a half or so before the 'Tommies' made their first fighting contact.

At Bentley Priory, Stanmore, headquarters of RAF Fighter Command, the Senior Controller of the Radar Filter Room, Wing

Commander M. Jarvis, came on duty shortly after 8 am that morning. His job was literally to filter all radar plots received and reported, especially those from south and south-east England, and then notify appropriate Group HQs, assuming anything important arised from such sightings. His attention was drawn to a plot of aircraft circling just near Le Havre, which Jarvis interpreted as Luftwaffe aircraft escorting coastal shipping. This plot had been received at Stanmore about 0930 hours and, since it persisted, Jarvis reported it and his interpretation to No 11 Group HQ at 10 am. Group HQ airily dismissed the plot as probably aircraft exercising.

At Biggin Hill airfield the controller there, Squadron Leader W.A.K. – 'Bill' – Igoe, also came on duty at 8 am, and on his first plots' check noticed a series of circular radar plots moving from the Cherbourg area, the larger blips apparently moving at a speed of at least 25 knots. Igoe, one of the few junior RAF officers who knew of *Operation Fuller*, was immediately suspicious. It was too fast a speed for any normal convoy or coastal shipping. Taking into account the aerial escort circling those large blips, Igoe concluded that they must be *Scharnhorst* and *Gneisenau*. He telephoned No 11 Group HQ and told them, 'I think it must be *Fuller*'. From the puzzled reply he got, Igoe felt that the chap at the other end had no idea what he meant by *Fuller*.

Bill Igoe, frustrated by the blank reaction yet hampered by his own inability to explain due to the security blanket imposed on all in the secret, used his own initiative and telephoned RAF Hawkinge to speak with Squadron Leader Bobby Oxspring of 91 Squadron. Without mentioning *Fuller* – damned security again! – Igoe asked Oxspring to 'go and look at some Hun fighters circling off the Somme Estuary and see what they're up to'. At 10.20 hours Oxspring and his No 2, Sergeant Beaumont took off from Hawkinge in their Spitfires on what seemed to be simply a 'special' *Jim Crow* sortie.

Only minutes before the pair got airborne Flight Lieutenant Gerald Kidd, station commander of Swingate airfield at Dover, began plotting three outsize blips on his radar screen, estimated these to be some fifty-six miles away towards Boulogne, and they roused his suspicions due to their abnormal size. After careful thought Kidd came to the positive conclusion that the blips could only mean one thing – the Brest battleships were in the Channel. The time was now 10.20 am. He tried to telephone a warning to Dover Castle, Admiral Ramsay's headquarters, to no avail – the GPO line was out of order. A further attempt on a secure 'scrambler' telephone line also failed to get through.

While Gerald Kidd struggled with the telephones, two more Spitfires were getting airborne from the tiny grass airfield at Kenley. The pilots were Group Captain F.V. Beamish, DSO, DFC, AFC, the base commander, and Wing Commander R.F. Boyd, DFC, the veteran leader of the Kenley Wing. Victor Beamish had decided to have a 'private looksee' around, hoping to meet some German prey, and Boyd was there primarily to keep a protective eye on the irrepressible Irishman.

At Swingate Flight Lieutenant Gerald Kidd finally managed to contact the Dover HQ, albeit via a roundabout telephonic link-up with Portsmouth, and duly reported his interpretation of his radar plots to Wing Commander J. Constable-Roberts, the air liaison officer on Admiral Ramsay's staff. 'Bobby' Constable-Roberts immediately contacted No 11 Group, only to receive the same lack of interest accorded to Bill Igoe, then telephoned No 16 Group HQ, Coastal Command at Thorney Island to suggest that No 42 Squadron's Bristol Beauforts and others should be sent to Manston as soon as possible. Once again he met a certain lack of urgent enthusiasm.

Sensing that he was unlikely to be able to initiate any positive reaction from either Fighter or Coastal Commands on his own authority, Constable-Roberts could now only rely on his boss, Admiral Bertram Ramsay to get things moving. Ramsay, a realist, had only one air striking force immediately available to him – Eugene Esmonde's 825 Squadron at Manston. To Ramsay the mere idea of ordering six ancient biplanes to attack such a formidable naval force was repugnant – it would be sheer suicide.

Picking up the telephone Ramsay got into direct contact with the First Sea Lord, Sir Dudley Pound, at the Admiralty. To his personal request not to be ordered to despatch the six Swordfish crews to a certain, and probably pointless death, Pound replied with a Nelsonian cliché, 'The Royal Navy will attack the enemy whenever and wherever he is to be found.' ...

Even as the various telephone conversations were underway, the pair of 91 Squadron Spitfires – Oxspring and Beaumont – were descending through cloud over the Channel, some fifteen miles west of Le Touquet. As they burst into relatively clear air they were immediately greeted with a flurry of flak shells from the German E-boat protective screen flanking the battleships, and saw a dozen Messerschmitt Bf 109Fs heading their way. Jinking rapidly through the flak and evading the German fighters, both Spitfires climbed swiftly into the rain-lashed cloud base for cover, noting at the same time three 'large ships' below them. Oxspring's initial reaction was that he'd stumbled upon a Royal Navy escort to an Allied convoy of some sort – the anti-aircraft fire was, after all, in accordance with the trigger-happy reputation (in the RAF) of all RN ships when approached by aircraft of *any* nationality.

Swinging through a driving rain across the ships Oxspring spotted two fighters slightly below him and promptly reefed round into an attacking position, followed closely by Beaumont. Closing to some 500 yards he was about to open fire when he realised they were Spitfires – he had crossed the flight path of Victor Beamish and Dicky Boyd. Warning Beaumont not to fire, Oxspring watched Beamish and Boyd dive towards the gaggle of shipping below for what appeared to be a strafing attack, then realised that the ships were almost certainly German, not RN. Since the purpose of his sortie was reconnaissance, not tackling large enemy ships probably bristling with heavy guns, Oxspring decided to return to base as fast as possible.

At that period No 11 Group, Fighter Command had in being a strict order for radio (R/T) silence for *all* pilots engaged on operations, an order signed by Group Captain Victor Beamish in his capacity of Senior Air Staff Officer (SASO) at 11 Group. Oxspring, though well aware of this order, was totally unaware of the *Fuller* plan, but considered that such a large enemy naval force so close to the English coast constituted a good enough 'emergency' for him to disobey the R/T silence order. Accordingly, he transmitted a message, 'Barman Blue Leader (his recognition code name for this sortie). Three large German ships, probably battle-cruisers, escorted by twenty-plus craft sailing off Le Touquet heading towards Dover'. He then told Beaumont to follow him back to base.

The German radio listening service (*Horchdienst*) picked up Oxspring's brief warning message and duly notified Adolf Galland at Le Touquet – yet no record of any RAF receipt of the warning appears to exist. Galland, with shrewd judgment of the English character in such situations, decided to do nothing about this apparent alert; he was prepared to believe that, assuming the RAF *had* received Oxspring's call, it would still take a long time for Allied defences to be brought into effective action – a judgment which was to prove entirely accurate.

Meanwhile Victor Beamish and his No 2, Boyd, had flown across the German ships' procession at almost deck level, then climbed hard to evade oncoming Luftwaffe fighters and gained cloud cover. Once there Beamish set course for Kenley to report his findings, maintaining his own authorised order of complete R/T silence en route. As one officer with actual knowledge of *Operation Fuller* Beamish might easily have broadcast the executive order '*Fuller*' over his radio and thereby saved precious time in getting British defences under way. Instead he stuck to his own orders – adding to the delay in countermeasures. At 10.50 am Oxspring and Beaumont landed back at Hawkinge and made their sighting report, with Beaumont adding that he was pretty certain that one of the large ships looked to him like the *Scharnhorst*.

Oxspring then spoke with Bill Igoe at Biggin Hill who, in view of his previous near-rebuff, suggested Oxspring ring 11 Group HQ direct and try to convince them of the battleships' presence in the Channel. On contact with 11 Group HQ, however, Oxspring and Igoe told that the AOC, Air Vice-Marshal Trafford Leigh-Mallory, was reviewing Belgian airmen at Northolt and ' ... was not to be disturbed'.

At 11.10 am Victor Beamish and Boyd landed at Kenley, and Beamish immediately tried to contact Leigh-Mallory with his news – only to be told that the AOC was 'unavailable'. Beamish persisted, refusing to merely leave a message with any of the various staff officers who answered his calls, and after almost half an hour Leigh-Mallory finally came to the Northolt telephone. An officer constantly highly conscious of his rank, and self-important to the point of pomposity on occasion, Leigh-Mallory was obviously very piqued by being 'summoned' to the telephone by a mere Group Captain, and it took the soft-spoken Beamish several minutes to calm his AOC down and to impress upon him the vital importance of his and the other Spitfire pilots' observations over the Channel. Once convinced, however, Leigh-Mallory immediately initiated the appropriate orders to execute *Fuller* in the context of No 11 Group's participation. The time by then was 11.35 am – another hour had been lost to the British defences since Oxspring's R/T broadcast.

For those immediately involved in *Operation Fuller* things started to move quickly from this point. Ramsay's Dover HQ received official confirmation of the identity of the ships in the Channel by 11.25 am, albeit via the 'channels' of 11 Group, RAF, Fighter Command HQ, Air Ministry, Admiralty. The various coastal artillery batteries along the south coast of England were immediately alerted, and at 12.10 hours the South Foreland battery commenced firing the first of 33 rounds of 9.2-inch calibre shells at the German naval force which by then had reached a point some ten miles west of Calais. None of these shells registered a hit on any ship.

Meanwhile, again acting on personal initiative, Victor Beamish telephoned Wing Commander Tom Gleave at Manston to tell him *Fuller* was 'on', while Wing Commander Constable-Roberts at Dover HQ had already spoken with Eugene Esmonde at Manston, warning him to be prepared in the very near future for take-off and to load the Swordfish of 825 Squadron with their torpedoes. Constable-Roberts, on receipt of full confirmation, then telephoned Fighter Command and 11 Group to request a strong fighter escort to be arranged as quickly as possible to escort Esmonde's Swordfish attack.

In the *Fuller* planning for any German breakout from Brest to take place by night through the eastern end of the Channel, it had been proposed to co-ordinate Esmonde's Swordfish attack with a simultaneous surface attack by destroyers and a total of thirty-two Motor Torpedo Boats (MTBs), thereby approaching the German ships by sea and air from several quarters and diffusing the full weight of opposing gunfire in any one direction. This combination of sixty-four torpedoes from the MTBs (two per boat) and the six to

(Left) Squadron Leader R.W. Oxspring, DFC. *(Right)* Squadron Leader Brian Kingcome, DFC, leader of the 72 Squadron Spitfires which escorted 825 Sqn, FAA on 12 February 1942.

'Stringbag' – Swordfish complete with torpedo. Note Light Series (LS) bomb carriers under wings.

be carried by the Swordfish, apart from any additional damage caused by the destroyers, could then be boosted by other surface attacks by other light RN forces, coastal guns, and further attacks by the Beauforts of Coastal Command and, if needed, up to 300 bombers from RAF Bomber Command.

In January 1942 such a force, based on the central premise of attacking at *night*, had seemed to be capable of trapping, even destroying any German attempt to run the Channel gauntlet. By early February, however, the naval forces were being reduced by Admiralty orders as, in its opinion, the emergency situation was receding. All destroyers and all but six of the MTBs were withdrawn from their immediate readiness status and dispersed, leaving merely the six MTBs commanded by Lieutenant-Commander Nigel Pumphrey based at Dover at 'four hours' readiness' by the morning of 12 February, with Pumphrey's own MTB *hors de combat* in dry dock having its fuel tanks exchanged.

That same morning Eugene Esmonde, on return from his Palace investiture, was up and about early, joining his crews for the daily two-hours' standby prior to dawn. On being stood down at dawn, the crews left their aircraft to take breakfasts in their respective Messes, then settled down to yet another day of training practices. It was a sharply cold morning, with frozen snow 'powder' whirling around the open airfield as a gusty wind stirred the wintry scene. In the wooden hut crew room allotted to 825 Squadron the operations notice board had been chalked up with details of crews and their aircraft for that day; while Swordfish W5983 was to take-off at 10 am for the first training flight of the day, a low-level torpedo-style exercise in Deal Bay by its crew of Sub-Lieutenant Brian Rose (pilot), Sub-Lieutenant Edgar Lee (Observer) and Leading Airman 'Ginger' Johnson, DSM as the rear gunner.

At that stage Esmonde was still under the impression that he and his crews would be undertaking a night attack as and if the *Fuller* balloon went up, and had therefore briefed and trained his crews accordingly. The prospect of such an attack, part-protected by the darkness hours, seemed wholly reasonable – dangerous, perhaps, especially in such slow biplanes, but by no means particularly so. His memory of the highly successful attack on the Italian fleet at Taranto by Swordfish at night might have given Esmonde sufficient example of what could be achieved even in the doughty old 'Stringbag' – the affectionate nickname for the Swordfish.

At 10 am, as ordered, Brian Rose and his crew left Manston and flew to Deal Bay to begin their training exercise. Many of the air and ground crews not needed immediately for training were off-duty, though remained on the station, occupying themselves in purely domestic matters. At the briefing hut one of the pilots, Charles Kingsmill, patiently waited to have his hair trimmed by the squadron 'barber'; others were taking the opportunity to write a letter home, see to their laundry, or simply sprawled in a variety of odd chairs reading and resting after their pre-dawn alert period of readiness.

For his part Eugene Esmonde was outside on an aircraft dispersal checking the torpedoes with his ground crews. To all intents 12 February looked very much like being just one more slightly boring day of routine duties.

CHAPTER TEN

No Better Way

At 11.30 am on the morning of 12 February the crews of six RN MTBs at Dover were resting after their early morning torpedo practice runs, waiting for their maintenance crews to finish fitting warheads to each MTB's pair of 'fish'. Officially the crews were standing by at four hours' readiness state, and two boat commanders had taken the opportunity to slip into Dover town on a quick shopping trip. Commander of the small force, Lieutenant-Commander Nigel Pumphrey, was in his office attending to routine paperwork when, at 11.35 am, the telephone rang. It was Captain Day, naval Chief of Staff to Admiral Ramsay at the Dover HQ: 'The German battle-cruisers are off Boulogne!'

Galvanised into action, Pumphrey banged the telephone down, ran to his operations room and yelled, 'Man all boats – *Scharnhorst* and *Gneisenau* are in the Straits!' Since his own MTB was in dry dock at that moment, Pumphrey took over command of *MTB 221* and its crew, and by 11.55 am was leading his five boats across the narrow harbour, heading for the open sea. The sea was choppy with a gusty westerly wind and some mist.

Fifteen minutes later, out of low misty cloud a small gaggle of German Focke Wulf Fw 190 fighters materialised over the MTBs, flying very low. Pumphrey ordered his gunners to open fire, and saw one Fw 190 shed pieces of metal from its wing, yet the Germans did not react and continued on their way.

Ahead Pumphrey could see smudged black smoke rising and within minutes visibility improved suddenly and he could see the German naval force some five miles away. The time was 12.23 pm and Pumphrey's signalman tapped out in Morse Code the signal, 'O-break-U', adding, 'Three battleships bearing 130 degrees, five nautical miles distance, course 70 degrees'.

Aboard *Scharnhorst* only minutes later Admiral Ciliax was handed a German translation of Pumphrey's dramatic signal − he now knew that after some fifteen hours' unmolested sailing he was finally to clash with the British Navy.

At the same time as Pumphrey received his 'action' order from Captain Day, another telephone call was made by Wing Commander Constable-Roberts from Dover Castle to Wing Commander Tom Gleave at RAF Manston, saying, 'The *Scharnhorst* and *Gneisenau* are out and approaching the Straits of Dover. Tell Esmonde'. Out at his squadron dispersal Eugene Esmonde looked up as a small Morris Minor car skidded to a stop on the runway, its driver yelling to him, 'You're wanted on the 'phone urgently, sir!'

Back in the briefing hut Esmonde heard Gleave tell him, 'The *Scharnhorst* and *Gneisenau* are approaching the Straits.' Replacing the receiver Esmonde gave orders for Brian Rose to be recalled immediately from his practice exercise, and for all 825 Squadron air crews to report at once. The TAGs, having a tea-break in the Sergeants' Mess then, rapidly made their way to the briefing hut, while Charles Kingsmill, halfway through his haircut, jumped off the chair and ran. Once gathered in the hut, the crews waited as Esmonde, still on the telephone, asked for news of the latest radar plotted location of the enemy ships.

A minute later Tom Gleave arrived in an ancient Ford V-8 car, to tell Esmonde that there was as yet no actual confirmation from the Admiralty. Then, at 11.40 am the telephone rang again, with Constable-Roberts saying, 'It's our friends all right, Group Captain Beamish has identified them off Boulogne'. Esmonde turned to his crews and in an unemotional tone told them to 'get ready'.

Meanwhile at Biggin Hill a confused gaggle of fighter pilots were gathering in the Watch Office, all asking Flight Lieutenant Cowan Douglas-Stephenson, the duty officer, why they had been called for. None had any idea, beyond the vague assurance that 'there was a flap'. Douglas-Stephenson was in no position to clarify the confusion − 'I knew that the battle-plan for *Operation Fuller* was in the locked safe, but the Intelligence Officer had gone on 24-hours' leave leaving the secret orders locked up, and no one could find the key'.

Finally No 11 Group HQ contacted the Biggin Hill controller,

Bill Igoe, giving him the go-ahead for a total of five fighter squadrons to prepare immediately to escort Esmonde's six Swordfish on their torpedo attack. Two squadrons from Hornchurch, Nos 64, commanded by Squadron Leader B.J. Wicks, DFC, and 411 RCAF, commanded by Squadron Leader R.B. Newton, DFC, RAF – for whom this date was actually his first day of command of 411 – would precede the Swordfish to smother any opposition flak from the German E-boat escorts to the battleships; while the other three squadrons were to stay with the Swordfish to beat off any Luftwaffe interference.

These three units were No 72 Squadron, commanded by the veteran Squadron Leader Brian Kingcombe, DFC based at Gravesend, and two units from Biggin Hill itself, Nos 124 Squadron commanded by Squadron Leader R.M.B. Duke-Woolley, DFC, and 401 Squadron RCAF, led by Squadron Leader A.G. Douglas, DFC, RAF. The lack of full briefing of these fighter pilots, combined with the last-minute haste in mounting the escort, led to near-complete confusion, total lack of co-ordination, and ultimately pure tragedy.

Exemplifying the haste and briefing omissions was the experience of Brian Kingcombe, leading ten Spitfires of 72 Squadron. An ex-Cranwell Cadet, Kingcombe had been one of the 'Few' of the Battle of Britain, and commanded 92 Squadron throughout the fighter offensive over France in 1941. On the morning of 12 February Kingcombe's squadron had been 'stood down' after breakfast – the cloudy rainy weather appeared to offer a 'scrub' of any operational flying. Then at 9 am the squadron was suddenly called from thirty minutes' 'Availability' to two minutes' 'Readiness', meaning all pilots were to be strapped in their cockpits, ready for take-off; the order coming from Bill Igoe at Biggin Hill. During the next three hours 72's men were 'released' from their cockpits on three occasions and wended their way to the nearby dispersal hut to relax, only to be ordered back again into their cockpits.

No reason was given to Kingcombe for this obvious flap, and Kingcombe was to remark later, 'I have never known anything so bloody silly as all that mystery about the *Gneisenau* and *Scharnhorst*.' When, at 12.18 pm, he received the eventual take-off ('Scramble') order Kingcombe was seated in his Spitfire, and was told, 'Get to

Manston to escort six Swordfish and intervene in a battle between German E-boats and British MTBs'. No mention was made of the German battleships, and Kingcombe could only wonder why the hell there was so much 'panic' about a 'small naval scuffle'. When he also heard similar instructions going to no less than four other squadrons he became even more puzzled – it had all the trimmings of something big, but where did the Swordfish and the MTBs come into the picture? Even as these queries flashed through his brain, Kingcombe was already bumping his way taxying out for take-off with the other nine 72 Squadron Spitfires dutifully trailing him.

At Manston, before any order had been issued to the five fighter squadrons, Eugene Esmonde waited patiently by a telephone in his briefing hut. He was waiting primarily for confirmation that his Swordfish would receive the projected fighter escort, though even if this transpired he still needed the exact location and speed of the German ships in order to finalise take-off time and course to set. The thought of leading his six young crews – the oldest of them scarcely twenty-five years old – on a daylight attack against half the might of the German navy appalled him. He had originally volunteered his squadron for *Fuller* on the premise of a night sortie, and indeed trained his men in the techniques necessary for such an attack. He knew only too well from personal experience what lay in store for his men now that it seemed certain to be a daylight attack.

As he agonised over the matter, the telephone rang again. It was No 11 Group HQ saying, 'We intend putting in the Biggin Hill Wing of three squadrons as top cover. The Hornchurch Wing of two squadrons will beat up the flak ships for you. Both Wings have been told to rendezvous over Manston. What time should they be there?'

Esmonde, with obvious relief in the tone of his voice, replied, 'Tell them to be here by 12.25 – and for the love of God get them to us on time'. He next sent an order to his crews to be ready for take-off but remained by the telephone; he still needed to know exactly where the ships were and therefore what course to set. It rang again – this time Constable-Roberts from Dover Castle, saying, 'The Admiral]*Ramsay*] wants to know how you feel about going in. He says it's to be your decision.'

Esmonde's reply was brief, 'Yes, the squadron will go in. Where is Jerry? What's his speed?'

Constable-Roberts came back to him, 'About ten miles north-east of the Straits sailing at 21 knots.' Then, in a quieter voice asked, 'Are you satisfied with the fighter escort? If so the Admiral says it's OK to go.' Then he added, 'Best of luck old boy'. Esmonde thanked him quickly and immediately studied his maps to work out the ships' likely position by the time he could reach them.

If Eugene appeared calm as he busied himself with the last-minute details of the projected attack, his inner turmoil seemed evident to the RAF controller in the briefing hut. As Esmonde had replaced the telephone after speaking with Constable-Roberts and turned to the map-strewn table, the controller had watched Esmonde's face. He recalls the feeling of shock as he looked at the little man – 'he looked like a man torn apart inside'.

Masking his inner feelings, Esmonde then addressed his crews in his usual incisive manner; 'We'll soon be going in, but forget all you've learned of a night attack. We'll attack in sub-Flights in line astern at a height of 50 feet. Intention; to hit and slow down any of the big ships. We'll have plenty of fighter cover so you won't have to worry too much about enemy aircraft. Once we're over the escort screens of destroyers and E-boats, attack independently. Pick your own target – but make *sure* it is *Scharnhorst*, *Gneisenau* or the *Prinz Eugen*. Now get to your aircraft, warm up and stand by.'

Perhaps typically, Esmonde omitted to finish his remarks with the customary 'Good luck' wish – perhaps he already felt that luck would play no part in what he was committing these youngsters to within the coming half-hour. As the eager crews bundled out of the room to make their way to their Swordfish, Esmonde completed dressing for the sortie, then after picking up his flying helmet began to leave, only to be stopped by the telephone ringing yet again. It was No 11 Group to tell him that the fighter escort might be a few minutes late. Esmonde replied crisply, 'We're taking off at 12.25. I'll orbit the coast for a few minutes.'

Tom Gleave met Esmonde as he started to walk to his aircraft and wished him luck. 'The look on his face shook me. It was the face of a man already dead. I'd known him as a vital man, alive and eager for anything. Now his eyes were dulled, his face grey, almost haggard. The sort of vacant, lifeless face you read about but never expect to see. He barely recognised me, although his mouth twitched automatically into the semblance of a grin and an arm lifted in a vague wave. It shocked me as nothing had done before nor has done since.'

Esmonde had by then been joined by Brian Rose and Edgar Lee, this pair having returned from their training exercise shortly before and been on their way to the officers' Mess when the rest of the squadron's air crews had passed them, yelling 'The balloon's gone up'. Racing back to the crew room they grabbed their flying gear and were told by Esmonde, 'Fly at 50 feet close astern of me. Attack independently once we're over the outer screen, then make your own way home.'

It was now 12.15 pm as the six crews clambered into their Swordfish, and as Esmonde was about to climb in to his own cockpit a runner arrived panting with a message from the control room, 'Dover says the enemy's speed is now estimated at 27 knots, sir'. Esmonde nodded his thanks and settled himself in his cockpit seat, strapping himself to the aircraft and plugging in his leads. Behind him in Swordfish W5984, 'H', his Observer Lieutenant W.H. Williams sat behind the cockpit coaming, while to Williams' rear in the open 'tandem' rear cockpit Leading Airman W.J. Clinton checked his single, hand-operated machine gun and ensured that the extra drums of ammunition were readily to hand.

Esmonde's mind must have been recalculating the location of his enemy targets in the light of that last-minute revision estimate of the ships' speed. It meant that precious time was slipping away, leaving him even less time to guarantee reaching the ships for any attack. Loaded with full crew and the torpedo, a Swordfish, even at full throttle, was unlikely to attain a speed higher than 90 knots.

Wasting no time he opened up the aircraft's engine and jerked forward, trundling down the slight slope of the eastern end of Manston's 'runway', turned and nosed into the icy wind, waiting a few moments to check that the other five Swordfish were OK and moving in behind him. Then, with a glance at the sky in the hope of seeing his promised fighter escort – there was no sign of it yet – Esmonde raised his right arm and waved the gloved hand, then began his take-off run. The time was 12.25 pm.

One by one the six laden Swordfish rumbled along Manston's

frozen grass 'runway' and lifted shakily into a wintry sky. In the lead was Eugene Esmonde's 'H', followed closely by the two other members of his first sub-Flight; Swordfish 'L' (W5907) piloted by Charles M. 'Pat' Kingsmill whose crew were Sub-Lieutenant R. McC 'Mac' Samples (Observer) and Leading Airman D.A. 'Don' Bunce (TAG), and Swordfish 'G' (W5983) skippered by Sub-Lieutenant Brian W. Rose, with Edgar F. Lee (Observer) and Leading Airman A.L. 'Ginger' Johnson, DSM (TAG).

The second sub-Flight following on were led by Swordfish 'F' (W4523) piloted by Lieutenant J.C. Thompson with his Observer Sub-Lieutenant R.L. Parkinson and TAG Leading Airman E. Topping. Behind Thompson came aircraft 'K' (W5985) with Sub-Lieutenant C.R. 'Timber' Wood (pilot), Sub-Lieutenant E.H. Fuller-Wright (Observer) and Leading Airman H.T.A. Wheeler (TAG); while the last Swordfish to leave was 'M' (W5978) captained by Sub-Lieutenant Peter Bligh – the winner of that coin-toss for this 'privilege' – and his crew of Sub-Lieutenant W. Beynon (Observer) and Leading Airman W.G. Smith (TAG).

Eighteen young men in six elderly biplanes off to challenge almost half the German navy, apart from a Luftwaffe force of (to the Swordfish crews) unknown strength. To Tom Gleave, standing on the airfield watching Esmonde and his men leaving, it was a moment charged with high emotion. Remembering the deathly hue of Esmonde's face back in the crew room, Gleave was convinced that the little Irishman *knew* his fate this day, and the mere thought of a man with such a conviction deliberately overcoming the ultimate fear all men felt, and still carrying out what he regarded as his plain duty, almost brought tears to Gleave's eyes.

As the Swordfish slowly passed him Gleave saluted each one – a final tribute. Gleave, in a later interview, said: 'Some sneer at fear – because they have never known real fear. Some sneer at emotion, too – I am not ashamed of it. Those Swordfish crews were courage personified – to me courage in the face of the worst of all fears is the supreme kind.'

As the Swordfish orbited the airfield picking up formation behind Esmonde, he levelled out at 1500 feet altitude and set course to Ramsgate to await the promised fighter escort. Passing eastwards across Manston the six aircraft passed under an evil-looking black cumulus cloud, and to Tom Gleave still watching them from below the effect of the cloud's shadow on the tiny formation, seemingly painting the Swordfish in black, was almost ominous. They reached Ramsgate by 12.29 pm and began to circuit the town, searching the skies for those vital fighter escorts; then at 12.32 ten Spitfires appeared, Brian Kingcombe and his men from 72 Squadron.

For two more minutes Esmonde continued orbiting hopefully – no more fighters were visible. It might be said that at this precise moment Esmonde decided his destiny. In view of the failure of the other four squadrons of Spitfires to rendezvous on time, as promised by Fighter Command and 11 Group, he could easily and logically have abandoned the whole sortie. No one could have blamed him had he done so. The situation was now completely different to that which had originally led him to volunteer 825 Squadron to participate in *Operation Fuller*.

It can only be speculation as to what passed through Esmonde's mind when, now, he realised that he and his faithful crews would be virtually on their own. Certainly, having already given his word to Constable-Roberts and Admiral Ramsay that his squadron would 'go in', Esmonde by his very nature would have felt totally obliged to honour his word – honour and duty had been the lynchpins of the Esmonde family lineage and Eugene particularly exemplified those ideals throughout his life. His devout Catholic faith undoubtedly softened the all-too human fear of death and its aftermath. But whatever his actual thoughts at that crucial moment, Esmonde's decision became instantly plain.

With a wave of his hand to the following Swordfish pilots, he set course from Ramsgate to the east, diving shallowly to a height of some 50 feet above the waves. The German ships, he calculated, should be some twenty-three miles away by now, and every minute lost would mean that they were speeding even further to safety. At their bare 85-90 knots forward speed it would take his Swordfish some fifteen minutes' flying to reach them and attack. There could be no more delay.

The facts of the 'missing' fighter escorts made a sorry tale of haste and inefficiency. Kingcombe's ten Spitfires had flown, by his own account, 'balls out right through the gate' and rendezvoused with Esmonde some ten minutes after take-off. The other two squadrons from the Biggin Hill Wing, Nos 124 and 401, led by Duke-Woolley, arrived at the rendezvous fifteen minutes late, found no Swordfish to escort, but set off eastwards and soon became embroiled in combat with German fighters. The two Hornchurch squadrons, Nos 64 and 411, collectively led by Group Captain Harry Broadhurst, did not arrive over Manston until 12.45 pm. From here they flew to the Calais area and ran into a few stray Messerschmitt Bf 109Fs from *Jagdgeschwader* 2, one of which Broadhurst later claimed as probably destroyed, but both units eventually returned without sight of the real objectives.

One other unit, not mentioned in 11 Group's promised escort, which was intended to aid the Swordfish sortie was 607 Squadron at Manston. Equipped with Hurricane IIB fighter-bombers, 607's normal tasks comprised cross-Channel daylight bombing and gunning strafes of German land installations, airfields *et al*. One of 607's Hurricane pilots at the time was Flight Sergeant J.W. Brooks (later, Flight Lieutenant, DFC, DFM) who recalled:

'About a week or so before the Channel Dash affair, Esmonde arrived at Manston with his six Swordfish and occupied the dispersal next to ours. Incidentally, they arrived long before we got wind of what they were doing on an RAF airfield. There was, naturally, a lot of friendly rivalry between the RN and the RAF, yet being all aircrew we always got on well together. The air gunners on the Swordfish shared our Sergeants' Mess and, although we talked together, we never found out exactly what they were supposed to be doing because they never went on ops and never mentioned what sort of job they were training for. It was during one of those training sessions that I met Esmonde. I was Duty Pilot one night, meaning I was in charge of the flare path and flying generally. Manston was a *Darky* airfield, its flare path consisting of oil-burning goose-necks carefully laid out into wind by the Duty Crew – there were no concrete runways at Manston then – and I as Duty Pilot was 'armed' with an Aldis Lamp. On this night Esmonde and his crews decided to do some practice nightflying, and Esmonde shared my lonely vigil for most of the night.

'It's difficult to recall accurately what we talked about, though as was natural for pilots, irrespective of rank, we must have got around to flying. I remember he asked me about shipping in the Channel – one of our jobs was bombing ships out there – and what I thought of enemy fighters. From our talk I got the impression that the RN were at Manston on detachment to have a go at some of the bigger ships which were sneaking up the Channel by night. One thing I did ascertain was that we were to do the escort for the Navy. There were two other Hurricane squadrons at Manston around that time; our sister squadron 615, and 3 Squadron which was engaged on night intruder work, although on occasion we all flew together e.g. on an emergency shipping strike.

'On the 'big day' [12 February] it seemed to start like any other day, because we weren't expecting anything to happen. Usually if we had a 'do' coming off we were briefed about it the evening before. This usually took place in a pub called the Walmer Castle in Westgate which was conveniently situated halfway between the Officers' and Sergeants' Messes. Later on that morning Ops rang up to tell us to 'Stand By' (also 615 and 3 Squadrons). It was a really miserable cold wet day with low cloud and visibility down quite low. Then we heard the news that half the German navy was steaming up the Channel. We also heard that the big guns at Dover were engaging, etc – though at times like that rumours were rife.

The upshot was that we took off at 12.40 hrs into the murk to escort the Swordfish, who flew in two Vics of three. It was very awkward for us because we couldn't get too far away from our charges as we'd have soon lost them in the very patchy mist and drizzle – clearing one minute then clamping right down the next. We also had the greatest difficulty in keeping *down* to their speed of little more than 100 mph. I could actually see our gunner friends waving to us from their rear cockpits. But it wasn't very long before we completely lost them, and confusion reigned whilst our little lot wandered around in the Channel at nought feet. It had been such a last-minute panic, with virtually no proper briefing, so we didn't quite know what was going on or what to do.

'Then we ran into the German fighters and had our work cut out defending ourselves, losing at least two chaps, Sergeants Walker and McLean. I saw a lot of ships though I don't think they included the *Scharnhorst* trio, being mostly flak ships i.e. small trawler types

armed to the teeth with anti-aircraft guns. Our squadron returned
home since we saw no point in being shot at. When we landed the
squadron was bombed up and another lot of pilots took what
aircraft were available to at least try to make a little impression on
those very cheeky German ships. The day then finished for me as
far as ops were concerned. In retrospect, my impression was that
the day was one big balls-up, and the Germans had caught us with
our pants down.'

As the six Swordfish flew away from the coast, Brian Kingcombe
took his squadron up to 2000 feet height slightly ahead of his
charges and began scanning the sky ahead. Not least of his
problems was maintaining contact visually with the biplanes; their
all-out speed of perhaps 90 knots meant that the Spitfire escort was
forced to fly a weaving pattern to reduce the collective forward
speeds, using minimum throttle. A combination of drizzling rain
and intermittent misty cloud was cutting maximum visibility to less
than four miles. Esmonde's leading sub-Flight was flying as he had
ordered in line astern, each Swordfish gently undulating some 50
yards apart, but Thompson's rear Vic had remained in arrow-head
formation. Esmonde himself appeared to be at full throttle because
Charles Kingsmill and Brian Rose were having difficulty in keeping
up with their commander – in itself a tiny example of the wide gulf
in pure experience between Esmonde and his subordinate pilots.

As they neared the halfway point of their flight towards the
German ships – roughly ten miles out from Ramsgate – two *Staffels*
of Messerschmitt Bf 109s of *Jagdgeschwader* 2, *Richthofen*,
commanded by Oberstleutnant Walter Oesau suddenly appeared
out of the mists from behind the wave-hopping Swordfish and
proceeded to attack, their cannon shells and bullets slashing along
the flanks of the biplanes. Most of the Swordfish sustained minor
damage to their fabric-skinned wings but no crew injuries. As the
Swordfish weaved to evade this surprise onslaught, Kingcombe's
Spitfires descended on the Messerschmitts and began to beat them
off towards Ramsgate.

Kingcombe's own recollection was: 'While making for a
Messerschmitt I suddenly saw a beautiful bloody battleship and I
thought to myself, "I never knew the Navy had such a lovely boat".
I was sure she was one of ours because she was heading straight for

Dover. Anyway, no one had told me anything about German battleships being in the Straits. Not realising she was only heading for the English coast because she was making a long zig-zag in evasive action, I went down to 600 feet to give her a signal. When everything opened up on me I was still not worried for I knew the Royal Navy fired at anything which appeared too near their ships. When I swung off, followed by the rest of the squadron, the air was suddenly full of German aeroplanes, mostly cannon-firing Fw 190s. They were nasty customers who had only come into service at the end of 1941, and were a little faster than the 109 Messerschmitts. As I tried to beat the German fighters off the Swordfish, which were still lumbering along, I realised that the "beautiful ship" was the *Prinz Eugen.*'

This first clash with the Luftwaffe air 'umbrella' to the German ships was brief, and Kingcombe quickly brought his Spitfires back over the Swordfish – his job was to protect the naval fliers, not chase after enemy fighters. Then, at 12.50 pm, they first saw their prime targets – a frightening array of huge battleships, sleek destroyers, and darting E-boats flashing along each side of the main naval procession. These latter were already putting out a dense smoke screen along the port flank of the main ship formation, but the most menacing aspect of what lay ahead of the Swordfish crews was in the air above the enemy ships. Layered from 50 to 2000 feet were a host of German fighters – to the inexperienced eyes of most of the Swordfish crews, a virtual armada of aircraft filling the sky in every direction.

The fighters were Messerschmitt Bf 109Fs of *Jagdgeschwader* 2, *Richthofen* and Focke Wulf Fw 190s from Major Gerhard Schopfel's *Jagdgeschwader 26, Schlageter,* – élite units of the Luftwaffe's fighter arm. These, in almost full strength, now concentrated on the approaching Swordfish. By now Esmonde's leading trio was less than two miles from the battleships, and were separated from Thompson's sub-Flight by almost half a mile. Dropping all flaps and undercarriages to reduce speed to match that of the Swordfish, the German fighters bore in for the kill with cannon and machine gun fire, virtually queueing in single file for a shot at 'those crazy Englanders'. Above them Brian Kingcombe was already bringing down his men of 72 Squadron to engage this latest onslaught:

'I went down to 100 feet, clipping the bottom of the clouds, and we managed to keep most of the German fighters off them. The Germans were firing heavy guns which threw up great mountains of spray like water-spouts. The Swordfish flew straight into them … The Fw 190s were swarming everywhere. I saw one go down after I had given him a burst. I claimed him, but unfortunately in the sudden "scramble" I had forgotten to take the cover off my camera – so I could not prove it. By this time it seemed as though there were a hundred fighters, both RAF and Luftwaffe, in the air.'

As the German fighters began what proved to be a massacre of the Swordfish, Esmonde had reached the outer destroyer and E-boat protective screen and plunged through the E-boats' smoke screen, on track still towards his prime objectives. Below him Nigel Pumphrey's five MTBs, only shortly before reinforced by a pair of Motor Gun Boats (MGBs), had completed their individual gallant attempts to torpedo the giant battleships, running through a holocaust of fire from E-boats, destroyers and, not least, close-quarter strafing from the closely attendant Fw 190s and Bf 109Fs. Each had fired its two torpedoes – though none registered a hit – and, now to all intents powerless to inflict any further damage, were rendezvousing at the south-east Goodwin Buoy. Their respective skippers decided to 'hang around' to watch what happened next, though some had in mind the distinct possibility that they might be needed to retrieve the crews of the Swordfish they had seen attempting to penetrate the outer screen defences of the German force – a propitious thought later to be the salvation of a few of those airmen.

Plunging into a latticework of red tracers and frightening geysers of water thrown up in his path by the heavy guns of the enemy battleships, Esmonde, his Swordfish already trailing tattered fabric from the initial clash with the Luftwaffe fighters, was followed closely by Brian Rose, with Charles Kingsmill's aircraft bringing up the rear of the leading sub-Flight. At that moment the German fighters bore in, running along the single file of the leading three Swordfish and blasting each in turn with cannon shells and machine gun bullets. The shock of this onslaught forced each Swordfish to weave violently to evade punishment, but soon each was back on course. In Kingsmill's own words:

(Right) Oberleutnant Egon Mayer of III/JG2, who shot down Esmonde and one other Swordfish on 12 February 1942. After scoring a total of 102 combat victories, Mayer was killed on 2 March 1944.

(Below) Focke Wulf Fw 190A-4 of II/JG2 at dispersal.

'I was not conscious of any danger. Esmonde kept steadily on course, the tracer criss-crossing all around him. I was oblivious of what was happening below and on either side. My whole attention was on Esmonde ... Fighters were screaming at us. The ships were throwing up a terrific barrage. But I was too intent on looking forward to notice (though behind me my Observer Reginald Samples and Gunner Donald Bunce must have thought they were flying through Hell itself). Apart from one glimpse of a German plane I don't think I took much notice of the Luftwaffe at all. And the noise of the engine drowned the roar of gunfire and the streams of bullets and cannon shells. The plane shuddered as flak and cannon shells thudded into it, but nothing took my gaze off Esmonde. Not then.

'Suddenly the whole picture was changed. Everything seemed to happen at once. I saw Esmonde's plane jerk upwards in the midst of the tracers and I knew it must have been badly damaged. Then in the confusion I lost sight of it.'

Ahead of Kingsmill and Rose, Esmonde's Swordfish became the focal point for the gunsight of Leutnant Egon Mayer of JG2 *Richthofen* and his wing-man Feldwebel Willi Stratmann. Their first run set Esmonde's aircraft tailplane afire and its TAG, Clinton, let go his machine gun and coolly clambered onto the fuselage back, eased his way towards the tail and began beating out the flames with his hands. Succeeding, Clinton edged his way back to his cockpit and resumed firing his single gun at the German fighters within range. Now the heavy guns of the *Prinz Eugen* – towards which Esmonde was valiantly attempting to fly – opened up, one shell neatly slicing away most of the Swordfish's port lower wing. The biplane staggered, dipped a wing towards the sea, yet recovered as Esmonde brought the doomed aircraft back on course, still heading towards the *Prinz Eugen*.

Then Mayer and Stratmann made one more pass, Mayer's fire killing Clinton and the Observer Williams, and smashing several bullets into Esmonde's back and head. The Swordfish was seen to nose up slightly, its torpedo fell away – apparently released on track for the *Prinz Eugen* by Esmonde's dying hand – then the shattered aircraft nosed down into the waves and disintegrated on impact. Mayer's fire also accounted for one of the other Swordfish of the leading trio – whether that of Rose or Kingsmill's is uncertain – while his No 2, Stratmann, claimed the third. Aboard the *Prinz Eugen* its captain, Helmuth Brinkmann, barked an order 'Port Fifteen!' and the ship easily evaded the approaching torpedo.

Esmonde's dying act was seen by Edgar Lee in the following Swordfish, while higher up a Spitfire pilot, Flight Lieutenant Michael Crombie, had watched fascinated when the gunner Clinton had crawled down the fuselage to extinguish the flaming tailplane. The sight so engrossed Crombie that he almost collided with a German fighter. Another witness to the slaughter of the leading trio of Swordfish was Brian Kingcombe, whose main impression was that these had probably been victims of the *Prinz Eugen's* heavy gunfire.

That Rose and Kingsmill, and indeed the second sub-Flight of Swordfish led by Thompson, had continued to fly into the veritable hell of gunfire and fighter onslaughts in the wake of Eugene Esmonde plainly exemplifies their faith in his leadership and, no less, the extraordinary powers of instinctive command Esmonde held over them. No one can ever know Esmonde's final thoughts as, dying from the bullets in his body, he continued his attack to the very last. Perhaps he found some solace in knowing that he had found that 'better way of passing into Eternity' …

CHAPTER ELEVEN

Survivors

When Mayer and Stratmann made their final deadly pass along the line of the leading three Swordfish, their fire not only killed Eugene Esmonde but also killed or wounded all but two of the nine crew men. In Brian Rose's aircraft, flying slightly behind Esmonde, the first bullets snuffed out the life of the gunner, 'Ginger' Johnson, as he faced the oncoming fighters with his puny single machine gun. When the crews had first climbed into their aircraft back at Manston, Johnson had asked of no one in particular, 'What flaming hell chance have we got?' – perhaps in his last minutes of life 'Ginger' had become resigned to his certain death on this sortie.

The same flurry of cannon shells flashed each side of Edgar Lee, miraculously without even scratching him, then burst the cockpit coaming behind Brian Rose and slammed red-hot slivers of exploding shells into Rose's back. Rose slumped forward under the shock of impact and the nose of Swordfish W5983 dipped towards the sea some 50 feet below. Lee, at that time looking forward waiting to sight their target, leaned over the shattered coaming and yelled in Rose's ear to pull her up. In a haze of pain Rose instinctively pulled back on the control column and the aircraft levelled out again.

Seconds later Lee watched in horror as Esmonde's aircraft heeled over and plunged to oblivion. Vaguely aware of a comparative silence behind him, Lee turned and saw Johnson slumped over his gun mounting, obviously dead. He tried to lift the gunner's body off the gun but Johnson's weight prevented this. With more German fighters boring in, Lee next stood up in his cockpit, facing rearwards, then began shouting directions to his pilot to be able to evade each attacker's fire.

Passing over the inner protective screen of destroyers, Rose – though racked with pain and his vision blurring – aimed the nose of his Swordfish at the first large ship he could see ahead – the *Gneisenau* – and waited for the moment he could release his torpedo in striking range. At slightly more than 1000 yards from his objective the aircraft suddenly bucked under the impact of a cannon shell which had pierced the aircraft's main petrol tank and exploded inside, releasing a stream of highly flammable aviation fuel. Though his strength was steadily draining away, Brian Rose managed to keep control of the waffling Swordfish, then, as Edgar Lee tapped his head and pointed at the emptying fuel gauge, Rose switched over to his reserve petrol tank. This would give him ten to fifteen minutes more flying if nothing else occurred.

Now, within 1000 yards of the *Gneisenau* (as Rose thought), he released his torpedo. Lee watched the 'iron fish' bounce on the waves, then settle in and begin its run, but on looking ahead again realised that that last damaging jerk of the aircraft had slewed the Swordfish off its original course, and they (and their torpedo) were in fact heading straight at the *Prinze Eugen*. Rose's weak voice announced his intention to get to the outer destroyer and E-boat screen, and asked Lee to give him directions.

Seconds later the sheer bulk of the *Prinze Eugen* loomed large directly over the Swordfish's nose – they were heading for a crash into the ship! Screaming at Rose to pull the aircraft up, Lee felt the Swordfish rise slightly as Rose responded, then they were crossing directly over the battleship. Narrowly scraping past one of the ship's masts, Lee looked down at the upturned faces of of *Prinz Eugen*'s gun crews for a fleeting second, then the aircraft was across – right in the middle of the German naval force.

Watching Brian Rose's struggle for survival was *MTB 44*, commanded by Lieutenant R.F. Saunders, who had earlier attacked the *Prinz Eugen* with torpedoes but failed to hit it. On retiring from the immediate battle area, Saunders had decided to wait nearby to see how the air attack went. He saw Rose's Swordfish fly over the *Prinz Eugen*, then dip and disappear into the sea, and immediately ordered his crew to make for the spot. Brian Rose, having negotiated the 'hurdle' of the battleship, was still alert enough to realise he only had a few minutes' flying fuel left, so warned Lee that he was going to ditch just outside the outer German destroyer screen, most of which had already left the scene eastwards. Holding the wallowing Swordfish firmly in a slight nose-up attitude, Rose put it down almost gently on the waves, then as it settled in the water, and his remaining strength ebbed away, the wounded pilot slumped back in his seat.

Edgar Lee immediately ripped the aircraft rubber dinghy out of its stowage, pulled its air toggle to inflate it, and threw it over the side of the fuselage after making it fast to the fuselage by its tie-cord. He next scrambled along the side of his cockpit attempting to lift the dead Johnson out, but the effort was too much for him. In the front cockpit Rose stirred, so Lee went to his aid as the befuddled pilot tried to extricate himself from his seat. Lee finally managed to get Rose over the side and into the dinghy, but as he was about to join him the Swordfish rolled sideways. Frantically working on the tie-cord knot, Lee cleared the knot only seconds before the aircraft, with an almost tired, creaking sigh, crumpled in mid-fuselage and slid into the depths, taking the body of Leading Airman A.L. 'Ginger' Johnson, DSM, RN with it to a permanent grave.

Edgar Lee's last sight of his companion aircraft, 'Pat' Kingsmill's W5907, was as Rose flew across and beyond the *Prinz Eugen*. He saw Kingsmill's aircraft, besieged by German fighters, apparently complete his torpedo drop, then bank unsteadily away towards the outer destroyer screen. For a second Lee felt a surge of pleasure to think that at least one of the Flight had made it, then his whole attention became concentrated upon the imminent ditching in the sea of his own aircraft. If Lee's fleeting view of Kingsmill's situation was slightly optimistic, for Kingsmill the thought of 'making it' just then was distinctly problematical. When the Luftwaffe fighters closed for their final killing attack both he and his Swordfish suffered punishment. His gunner, Donald Bunce, crouching down behind his machine gun, kept up a series of snap bursts as each fighter approached despite the visible hail of fire passing all around him.

A momentary lull in the onslaught caused Bunce to stand up to see where the next one was coming from, but when he tried to sit down again he found that his tiny seat and a large chunk of the under-fuselage beneath him had simply disappeared – one burst of cannon shells had ripped away the bottom half of his end of the cockpit leaving Bunce with an uninterrupted view of the sea some fifty feet away. The same hail of shells passed 'Mac' Samples and sliced away two of the aircraft engine's cylinders. Kingsmill recalled that moment:

'There was a sharp blow on my shoulder and I knew I was hit. Yet strangely I felt no pain. Almost at the same time there was a deafening roar in my ears. Samples was bellowing down the speaking tube, "To port, for God's sake!" Frantically I whipped the plane sideways as tracers headed straight for us. In the next few seconds I jigged violently to avoid the stuff they were throwing up. I didn't know until later that Samples had been frantically trying to get my attention for nearly half a minute. When I didn't respond he realised that the speaking tube had been severed by fire, and he had to grope to find the broken end to shout through …'.

By then Kingsmill was flying over the outer edge of the German destroyer screen which began putting up a furious barrage. To Bunce and Samples, however, the German fighters remained the prime danger and, in their intense excitement both men were standing screaming obscenities at the oncoming fighters and gesturing with two fingers in the universal Service indication for their tormentors to ' … off!' Seconds later another burst of cannon shells hit the fuselage between Samples and Kingsmill, wounding both men, yet leaving Bunce unscathed. Kingsmill recalls:

'He [Samples] was still guiding me through the fire when something thudded into my thigh. A second later flak smashed my foot. But I still felt no pain. I seemed to be numb to everything. Yet I can remember praying, "Don't let me get hit in the head or I'll lose control … anywhere but my head … ".'

Samples felt a sudden burning sensation in his leg and on looking down at his flying boots was shaken to see a neat cluster of holes in one boot. His mind refused to understand this for a second, then he saw blood oozing out of the holes – he'd been hit! The unreality of it still remained; he could feel no pain, only curiosity. Looking around him at his aircraft Samples could see some of the damage already inflicted by the enemy fire; long jagged holes in the fabric covering of wings and fuselage, with tattered, scorched fabric strips dancing crazily in the slipstream – it was a minor miracle they were still airborne. Glancing ahead through the mist of smoke of battle

Samples could see a particularly large ship. It was the *Prinz Eugen*, some 2,000 yards away, with (it seemed) dozens of guns all firing directly at the Swordfish.

Kingsmill continued:

'We were still flying, straight towards the enemy in a plane becoming more difficult to handle with every second. I never grasped then just how smashed up we were; we'd been riddled in dozens of places. There was a huge splash in the sea close by. They were throwing their big stuff at us now – laying 11-inch shells in our path, hoping to smash us down before we reached firing distance ... now we must be almost there. I wrenched at the controls, brought the tattered Swordfish into firing position. Looming out of the mist was one of the target ships – the *Prinz Eugen* – which looked enormous. Somehow I lined the plane up against her. Everything was so confused that I cannot even remember pressing the torpedo release, but with the torpedo gone we stood some chance of getting out in one piece. The controls were dreadfully sluggish, but I brought the Swordfish around and yelled for Samples to give me a course back. As I came round and away I had a fleeting glimpse of the second Flight just above me, heading for the welter of fire I was trying to leave.'

Kingsmill's intention at that point was to fly back to England, but Samples more realistically pointed towards some light ships which he thought were the British MTBs and told Kingsmill to ditch alongside them. Kingsmill, accordingly, headed the aircraft over these boats, only to be greeted with furious flak – they were a section of the German E-boat protective screen. Samples received a further wound in his bottom, and yet more holes appeared in the aircraft's wings. The battered Swordfish was by now incapable of any normal violent evasive action, but Kingsmill achieved the 'impossible' by deliberately putting it into a flat turn. It worked – he dodged the worst of the flak and was soon out of the gunners' range.

Reduced to near stalling speed, the Swordfish would obviously fall out of Kingsmill's control at any minute, and he searched the sea desperately for something which might help. Suddenly he was deafened by a series of explosions and dazzled by ultra-brilliant lights bursting all around him. The aircraft's stowed distress signal cartridge pyrotechnics had detonated, and the aircraft now presented a somewhat fantastic sight – lurching along at almost wave height, trailing myriad ragged fabric 'streamers', gaping holes in virtually every part of its wings, fuselage and tail, and now spewing a veritable Brock's benefit of dazzling red fireworks in arcs in all directions. Inevitably some of the burning cartridges struck parts of the Swordfish as they detonated, one setting fire to the wing-stowed aircraft dinghy. No more than a minute later the Swordfish finally gave up the unequal struggle to remain airborne. In Kingsmills' words:

'Still holding the stick against me with all my strength we ended by flying literally into a wave, landing tail down. I heaved myself out of the cockpit and walked slowly down the rocking fuselage to the tail, then stepped into the sea. Samples and Bunce scrambled out to join me. "Shouldn't be long", Samples gasped out weakly, "I saw a motor-boat and signalled with the Aldis Lamp before I got clear".'

'Mac' Samples had been lucky to survive the ditching. He had failed to remember that he was still tied to his cockpit by a G-String – the strap usually fixed to his body to prevent him falling out of his cockpit should the aircraft do anything violent in manoeuvre. Thus, when the Swordfish began to sink into the sea Samples was dragged down with it, and it was some time before he managed to extricate himself and surface, near-drowned.

A nearby British ship had spotted Kingsmill's descent – it could hardly have missed the inadvertent Guy Fawkes display of the exploding pyrotechnics – and within fifteen minutes it drew alongside the trio of floating airmen. Rope climbing nets were dropped over the side of the ship and Donald Bunce started trying to help the badly wounded Samples to climb up the net. Then several of the ship's crew jumped into the icy sea to assist them, and eventually hauled Samples and Kingsmill onto the deck, while the unwounded Bunce managed to climb unaided. Once aboard all three were immediately wrapped in blankets – apart from the ordeal of exposure in the below-zero temperature of the sea, each man was beginning to undergo a form of secondary shock after their experiences of the past hour or so. 'Mac' Samples was laid down on the deck of the ship, unable to stop a constant shivering, and well recalled the well-meant intentions of a somewhat hefty member of the ship's crew who decided to literally lie on top of him and thereby warm Samples; an intention rather spoiled for 'Mac' when said sailor had to leave him on several occasions in order to be sea-sick over the ship's side! Once having retrieved Kingsmill and his crew, the ship then continued, in company with *MTB 44*, in searching the sea for further Swordfish crew survivors.

The only other survivors the ships were to find were Edgar Lee and Brian Rose. Once aboard their tiny dinghy, Lee and the badly wounded Rose attempted to bail out water from it. Rose's left arm was unusable, but even in his parlous condition he still tried with his other arm to help Lee with the bailing. Quite soon the sea became rougher as the weather conditions deteriorated, pitching the fragile rubber dinghy at perilous angles as it rode the waves. High above them Lee could see and faintly hear the escalating aerial battle between the Luftwaffe fighters and the RAF. Suddenly, as the dinghy topped one wave, a burst of tracer bullets whipped over Lee's head. Off to starboard were several German E-boats bringing up the rear of the German naval formation, and their gunners had decided to fire at the unknown yellow object bobbing about.

Pulling Rose down, Lee sheltered his wounded pilot while the firing lasted, then began the wearying process of bailing out shipped sea water again. In the dinghy's survival pack were several distress signal red cartridges and an aluminium sea marker cartridge. While mentally reserving the distress cartridges until things got really desperate, Lee decided to operate the sea marker – a container filled with aluminium silver fine powder which, when tipped into the sea, would form a brilliant silver patch all around the dinghy to mark their position for any air or surface searchers. In his haste, however, Lee committed the cardinal naval sin of tossing the contents *into* wind – and immediately both he and Rose received a liberal 'coating' of silver powder on themselves ...

Unbeknown to Lee, his dinghy had already been spotted from the air by a Spitfire pilot, Pilot Officer Rutherford, who after a clash with some Fw 190s, one of which he shot into the sea, came down low over the sea and spotted the half-submerged yellow-orange dinghy. Rutherford promptly transmitted three 'May-Day'

(Above) Reginald McCartney – 'Mac' – Samples, DSO.

(Left) Charles – 'Pat' – Kingsmill (left) and 'Mac' Samples recovering from wounds received on 12 February 1942.

signals at minute intervals to pinpoint the dinghy to anyone listening on his wavelength, then returned to the aerial struggle higher up. Meanwhile Lee and Rose were beginning to suffer from exposure to the freezing wind and water, and Lee had to keep prodding, even punching the semi-conscious Rose to stop him succumbing to an overwhelming desire to sleep.

Finally, after some two hours on the sea, Lee decided it was time to use the distress signal cartridges. His signal was spotted by *MTB 44*, which had been sweeping the area for more than an hour, but as the MTB hove in view of Lee he was convinced it was an E-boat and remained silent; depressed at the thought that after all he and Rose had been through they were about to become prisoners of war. Only as *MTB 44* drew alongside the dinghy, and Lee realised that they were English voices shouting to him, did he feel a warm wave of utter relief. One of the MTB's crew jumped into the sea and fastened the dinghy alongside the boat, then helped to lift the exhausted airmen aboard. Both were taken below deck, swaddled in blankets, and given stiff tots of rum – one particular type of grog which Edgar Lee happened to detest ...

Lee and Rose were picked up shortly after 3 pm, and by dusk all five surviving Swordfish crew men had been returned to England, where, after further restorative first aid, Rose, Kingsmill and Samples were admitted to hospital for surgical treatment of their wounds – an experience highly embarrassing for the youthful 'Mac' Samples, who had to undergo the blush-making process of having the E-boat flak pieces removed from his bottom in front of several female nurses!

Edgar Lee, after suitable treatment, was taken to Dover Castle to report personally to Admiral Ramsay, who sat grim-faced and visibly moved as he listened to Lee's account of the horrors he had experienced only hours earlier. Then, late in the evening, Lee was transported back to RAF Manston, along with the only other unwounded survivor, Donald Bunce. Back at Manston, Bunce summed up the whole afternoon's activities succinctly in his log book: 'Torpedo attack against *Scharnhorst* and *Gneisenau*. Attacked by fighters (Fw 190s) and forced into sea.'

For Edgar Lee his return to the Officers' Mess at Manston was an emotional experience, and his appearance was greeted in a hushed silence as those present realised that he was the only one of eighteen young men who had left the airfield to walk back, being unaware as yet of the other four survivors' rescue.

What of the second sub-Flight, so resolutely led by Thompson? These three Swordfish, in a tight Vee-formation, had last been seen by Kingsmill heading determinedly into the hell of flak and fighters of the German outer protective screen to the battleships. Their fate had been swift. As all three emerged inside the screen they were massacred by Focke Wulf Fw 190s from *Jagdgeschwader* 26, led by Oberleutnant Johannes Naumann of *Staffel* III, whose account read: 'I saw three Swordfish in 'V' formation heading for the battle-cruisers. I took the leader in a head-on pass and he crashed straight into the sea with his torpedo still attached.' Naumann then shot down a second Swordfish, while the remaining Swordfish fell to the guns of an unidentified German pilot of the same *Gruppe*. The whole 'combat', – if such it could be called – lasted some three minutes. None of the nine Swordfish crew men was ever seen again. In his official report later, Admiral Ciliax was to claim:

> According to reports from the leader of the Luftwaffe formations overhead, the first air wave is arriving and consists of eight (*sic*) torpedo-carrying planes with 18-20 (*sic*) Spitfires. Under pressure of the German fighters the torpedoes are released from a great distance, seemingly without target. The Luftwaffe is responsible for shooting down three aircraft, the *Scharnhorst* for one, and *Prinz Eugen* for three of the four bombers which directly attacked the ships.

In the mist, murk, and keyed-up tension of the moment, such discrepancies in details are patently unavoidable. While the three Swordfish credited to the Luftwaffe by Ciliax undoubtedly refer to Thompson's second sub-Flight, the main differences between Ciliax's second-hand evidence – he was aboard the *Scharnhorst* at the time and therefore not in *direct* contact with the actual Swordfish attacks – and the after-combat reports of Egon Mayer and his No 2, Stratmann, leave little doubt that the first three Swordfish

(Esmonde's Flight) were the victims of JG2. Mayer was by then a veteran *Experte* ('ace') with more than thirty confirmed aerial combat victories credited to him; not a man given to exaggeration or 'glory hunting', but methodical, even clinical in his regard for his profession.

CHAPTER TWELVE

Honour The Brave

On his return to RAF Manston Edgar Lee was met by Wing Commander Tom Gleave, who silently clasped Lee's hand, being unable to find any suitable words of solace for this fresh-faced youngster who had just returned from a private hell in which thirteen of his friends had died and three others were now maimed in hospital. Instead Gleave returned to his office to compile his report on the day's operational activities. Once in the privacy of his office, Tom Gleave, a hardened veteran fighter pilot who had himself been scathed in the fiery crucible of aerial warfare, wept openly as he recalled the sight of Eugene Esmonde and his young, eager air crews as they had mounted their Swordfish aircraft only a few hours before. In the outer office his WAAF clerk was also weeping for her boy-friend, one of those naval airmen.

Gathering his thoughts together, Gleave then drafted his report. When he came to the part played by 825 Squadron FAA, he wrote:

Concerning pilots and crews of 825 Squadron which operated from Manston against *Scharnhorst*, *Gneisenau* and *Prinz Eugen*, attached is the report of Sub-Lieutenant Lee. As Officer Commanding this station to which 825 Squadron was attached for operational purposes, and having been fully acquainted with their operational activities and the circumstances attendant thereto in respect of the above operation against enemy warships, which resulted in the loss of the entire squadron and seventy-five per cent of their crews, I respectfully submit that it would not be presumptuous on my part to express an opinion on the manner in which Lieutenant-Commander Esmonde and the crews under his command carried out their duties on this occasion.

(Left) Edgar Lee, a photo taken on 13 February 1942, the morning after his ordeal.

(Below) Edgar Lee talking with Wing Commander Tom Gleave on the morning after 825 Sqn's sortie, outside the Westgate Officers' Mess, Manston.

I discussed the operation with Lieutenant-Commander Esmonde prior to the squadron taking off at 12.30 [*sic*]. His pilots and crews present at this meeting displayed signs of great enthusiasm and keenness for the job they were about to undertake, and it was no doubt due to Lieutenant-Commander Esmonde's leadership that such a fine spirit prevailed. Nothing more was heard of the squadron until the five survivors were brought ashore. The German battle-cruisers were undoubtedly protected by a terrific barrage of flak, and covered by one of the biggest fighter screens ever seen. Against this, the determination and gallantry shown by Lieutenant-Commander Esmonde and his pilots and crews is beyond any normal praise. I am of the opinion that Lieutenant-Commander Esmonde is well worthy of the posthumous award of the Victoria Cross.

Gleave's recommendation that Esmonde be awarded a VC was without precedent – an RAF officer recommending a naval officer for the supreme award had no parallel in the long history of the little bronze cross. Gleave's report was addressed to the AOC, No 11 Group, RAF Fighter Command, Leigh-Mallory, who duly 'endorsed' the recommendation and passed it to the Admiralty for consideration.

Gleave's total admiration for Esmonde and his crews was matched by several of the men aboard the German ships which had been the targets for the Swordfish attack. Wilhelm Wolf, a young junior officer aboard *Scharnhorst*, thought of the Swordfish attack in somewhat theatrical terms: 'What an heroic stage for them to meet their end on. Behind them their homeland, which they have left with hearts steeled to their purpose, is still in view.'

To *Scharnhorst*'s 42-year-old navigator Helmuth Giessler, such devotion to duty was wholly moving: 'Such bravery was devoted and incredible. One was privileged to witness it ... They knowingly and ungrudgingly gave their all to their country and went to their doom without hesitation.' To Kurt Hoffmann, captain of *Scharnhorst*: 'It is nothing but suicide for them to fly against these big ships.' Admiral Ciliax, when writing up his war diary next day, described the Swordfish attack as: 'The mothball attack of a handful of ancient planes, piloted by men whose bravery surpasses any other action by either side that day.'

Admiral Bertram Ramsay, from his Dover Castle HQ, signalled the Admiralty: 'In my opinion the gallant sortie of these six Swordfish constitutes one of the finest exhibitions of self-sacrifice and devotion that the war has yet witnessed.' Having thus expressed his heartfelt view of 825 Squadron's sacrifice, Ramsay then proceeded to make known his equally honest views on the chaotic disorganisation and inefficiency which had led to the deaths of Esmonde and his men in a personal message to the FAA station at Lee-on-Solent, the official base of 825 Squadron:

> I cannot help but regard the miscarriage of the plan to provide fighter escorts for the Swordfish as a major tragedy of this war. Until the time they took off I had thought all arrangements were proceeding satisfactorily. Had I known that the fighter escorts might not keep their rendezvous I would have told Lieutenant Commander Esmonde to remain on the ground; indeed, I would have forbidden the flight as an order.

It was the first of a swiftly mounting wave of recriminations and reproaches to be voiced at all levels of public and official participation over the preliminary and actual operational planning and execution of *Operation Fuller* over the coming weeks. Within the hallowed walls of the Admiralty – far from the smoke of battle – a distinctly sanguine opinion was recorded of Eugene Esmonde's fateful decision to fly the sortie: 'He was free to act as he thought best and believed he might succeed. That he was taking tremendous risks he knew, but was prepared to face them, as he had faced other risks many times before.' Though possibly well-intentioned, this view was the subject of sharp, even heated criticism later by men who were closer acquainted with the man and the circumstances he found himself bound by that morning of 12 February 1942.

Tom Gleave's original recommendation that a posthumous VC should be awarded to Eugene Esmonde found approval, and the *London Gazette* of 3 March 1942 announced the award. Its citation read:

On the morning of Thursday February 12, Lieut-Commander Esmonde, in command of a squadron of the Fleet Air Arm, was told that the German battle-cruisers *Scharnhorst* and *Gneisenau* and the cruiser *Prinz Eugen*, strongly escorted by some 30 surface craft, were entering the Straits of Dover and that his squadron must attack before they reached the sandbanks north-east of Calais. Knowing that his enterprise was desperate, Lieut-Commander Esmonde and his squadron of six Swordfish set course for the enemy shortly after noon and after ten minutes' flying were attacked by a strong force of enemy fighters. The fighter escort was lost and in the action which followed all the Swordfish were damaged, but he flew on against hopeless odds, and was met by intense fire from the battle-cruisers and their escort. The port wing of his Swordfish was damaged, but Lieut-Commander Esmonde led his squadron straight through the fire from the ships in steady flight towards their target. Almost at once he was shot down but the squadron went on and launched a gallant attack in which at least one torpedo is believed to have struck the battle-cruisers and from which not one of the Swordfish returned. His high courage and splendid resolution will live in the traditions of the Royal Navy and remain for many generations a fine and stirring memory.

Of the remaining seventeen men of 825 Squadron, the five survivors were also decorated; Rose, Kingsmill, Lee and Samples each being awarded a Distinguished Service Order (DSO) – an unusual occurrence for such junior officers to receive this 'senior' award – while Donald Bunce, the sole surviving non-commissioned airman, received a Conspicuous Gallantry Medal (CGM), in itself a relatively rare award. Under the contemporary ruling in matters of awards and decorations within the British Armed Services only two gallantry awards could be recommended *and* awarded *after* a Serviceman's death in action – the Victoria Cross and a 'Mentioned in Despatches'.* The latter was (is) a small bronze oak leaf emblem

---

* The George Cross, instituted on 24 September 1940, could also be awarded posthumously, but was created as a civilian award.

which could be sewn across the ribbon of any campaign medal, or simply sewn directly onto a tunic or jacket in lieu of any such particular ribbon.

Accordingly, and in strictly bureaucratic adherence to the book, each of the remaining twelve men of 825 Squadron who died on 12 February 1942 were merely listed as 'Mentioned in Despatches'. This decision infuriated many Servicemen associated with *Operation Fuller*, not least Wing Commander Tom Gleave who now bitterly regretted that he had not recommended more of those FAA crews for a VC. 'Mentioned in Despatches' awards, though to a large extent granted for outstanding services under operational conditions, were almost equally earned by administrators and other non-combatant Servicemen and women far removed from any bullets fired in anger, and in certain cases had become virtual ration awards for senior officers and other personnel. To lump such recipients with the self-sacrifice and courage displayed by the dead crews of 825 Squadron seemed to most Servicemen bordering on insult.

The announcement of the award of a posthumous VC to Eugene Esmonde was received with pride by his family. Of Eugene's immediate relatives, his beloved mother Eily still lived in the family home Drominagh, though she was now part-invalided by arthritis and relied heavily in day to day routine upon a wheelchair purchased for her by Eugene. The eldest brother Owen was still an RAF officer, stationed in early 1942 at Rotherham; while the youngest brother Patrick –'Paddy' – was serving as a captain with the RAMC. Witham Esmonde was with the Royal Navy, and Eugene's sister Carmel was a humble ACW in the WAAF, serving 'down the hole' at RAF Uxbridge. Patrick, serving at the time in Penzance, Cornwall, heard the news of Eugene's award over the radio and immediately thought of his bereaved mother Eily, and the possible consolation this news might bring her in her sorrow over Eugene's loss. Consulting with Owen and Carmel, Patrick received their ready agreement that if it was at all possible to arrange Eily Esmonde should be the one to actually receive Eugene's VC at the forthcoming royal investiture, on 17 March – St Patrick's Day – a date specifically suggested by HM King George VI for his personal presentation of the cross to the Esmonde family.

The problem now was how to actually arrange transportation of Eily from neutral Eire to a wartime Britain. Patrick decided to tackle the Admiralty, arriving in London on 1 March and being directed to the office of a Miss Watts, a civil servant within the Admiralty administration. Miss Watts listened sympathetically to Patrick's explanation of his mother's invalid circumstances, then immediately took charge of the situation, promising Patrick that suitable transport would be arranged, and that meantime he should see his mother and get her own agreement to come to London.

On 2 March Patrick arrived in Dublin where he joined Carmel, and next day both drove to Drominagh. After obtaining Eily's assent to attending the investiture, Patrick and Carmel returned to Dublin, and Patrick telephoned Miss Watts at the Admiralty to confirm his mother's agreement. Miss Watts in turn informed Patrick that an FAA aircraft was to be placed at the family's disposal, a De Havilland Dominie, the personal aerial 'hack' of the Fifth Sea Lord – an unprecedented arrangement for any naval aircraft to be placed at the use of a civilian having no part in military, naval, or political activities. That such an arrangement was so quickly made speaks volumes for the influence and determination of Miss Watts, apart from an understandable desire by the Admiralty to do everything possible to honour the memory of the Fleet Air Arm's sole VC.

Returning to London on 9 March, Patrick was informed that the Dominie which was to fly his mother to England was, at that time, in Scotland and would pick him up at Chester on 14 March for the flight to Belfast, and that it would be piloted by a former FAA colleague of Eugene, Lieutenant-Commander Sir George Lewis. After picking up Patrick, Lewis set off across the Irish Sea bound for Belfast but ran into atrocious weather conditions, forcing him down to land on the Isle of Man. An hour later Lewis continued his flight but on approaching Belfast he was warned of an air raid alert then under way, and advised to land further north of the city.

After landing both men changed quickly into civilian clothing – Eire was strictly neutral – and travelled by train to Dublin, and next morning Patrick drove to Drominagh to join his mother and sister Carmel, then drove them back to Dublin and took the next train to Belfast, finally arriving at the airfield north of the city where George Lewis and his Dominie were waiting, ready for take-off. Here they met another minor problem – Eily's wheel-chair could not be stowed in the aircraft and would have to be left behind. A major anxiety for all was the continuing bad weather, but Lewis, highly conscious of the time element – it was now 16 March, the day before the investiture – decided to take off anyway. Patrick's own description of the flight was:

'So we took off on the 16th at 1pm – Mother, Carmel and myself, with Sir George piloting with a crew of two. It was very bumpy and we could hardly see the ends of the wings. My eyes were, of course, on Mother – how was she going to react to this very unpleasant flight? This, coupled with the thought that George might turn back at any moment, gave me plenty to think about.

'I soon discovered that Mother was by far the least concerned of the six of us in that plane, and that George, having set course for England, intended staying on it. We plodded onwards and eventually, at three o'clock, landed at Chester. Then George decided to fly on, low through the valleys, to London. Once again he made it successfully through very bad weather and we landed at Hendon at five. A magnificent car drew up alongside the plane – the Fifth Sea Lord's personal car – and by six o'clock we were in London drinking tea at the Welbeck Hotel. Mother had taken the long journey from Ireland wonderfully and seemed quite surprised when everyone asked her if she was tired.'

Joined at the hotel by Owen Esmonde, the family retired early in preparation for the next day's investiture. Next morning at 10 am, all wearing a shamrock, Owen, Patrick and Eily went to Buckingham Palace, only to be stopped at the Palace gates by a duty constable who told them that only two people at a time were permitted to go before the King, but on learning their identity the policeman promptly let them through and they proceeded slowly through the courtyard to the entrance door. Here Patrick spoke with a sergeant of the Palace's Home Guard who, as if by magic, immediately produced a comfortable bath chair for Eily. Assisted by two more Home Guards, Patrick and Owen carried Eily in her chair into the Palace and came into a beautifully furnished long hall filled with chairs and many other people waiting to be called

Eily Esmonde holding Eugene's Victoria Cross, with her sons Owen (left) and Patrick, outside Buckingham Palace, 17 March 1942.

before the King. Patrick takes up the story again;

'We were put in the front row as Mother was to be the first to go up. A Marine major came up and spoke to Mother, saying he regretted that only one of us would be allowed to go up with her. After hearing the circumstances, he volunteered to ask the King if we could both accompany Mother. This he did and the King apparently agreed, for we were told by the major that both of us could go up with Mother.

'This was entirely an investiture for next-of-kin, and I suppose there were about 200 people to represent 100 heroes. Next to us was a senior Army Chaplain and his VAD daughter, there to receive his son's George Cross – a Wing Commander who had been killed in Malta. Amongst those 200 people I never saw one cry. At about 10.30 an Admiral, who had already spoken once to Mother, gave us a short talk on the procedure – I'm nearly sure he was Evans of the *Broke*. Now we were all in rows along the length of this magnificent hall, and facing us in the centre was a large door. It was through this door that the King had to enter at eleven o'clock. As Mother was to be the first up, we were told to wheel her in her chair to about ten yards from this door so that she would be ready as soon as the King came in. Owen pushed the right-hand side and I the left. When the King entered everyone stood. He was dressed in naval uniform, and he asked us all to sit down.'

After Eugene Esmonde's VC citation had been read out, Patrick and Owen wheeled their mother forward, then stood stiffly at attention a pace behind her chair. King George VI stepped forward, then bent down to shake Eily Esmonde's hand gently. Expressing his sorrow at Eugene's gallant death, he recalled that it had only been a few weeks since he had personally given Eugene his DSO award. With a final word of sympathy to Eily, the King next straightened up and shook hands with Owen and Patrick. In her wheel-chair Eily cradled the tiny box containing Eugene's bronze cross which the King had handed to her – it seemed so small, yet so precious ... As the King stepped back Owen and Patrick wheeled Eily back behind the rows of chairs. There each in turn followed their mother's example in kissing the cross, murmuring 'For Eugene'.

A few hours later all boarded the Dominie again and, in clear, bright skies, began the long journey back to the peace and solitude of Drominagh; back to the house, woods and shimmering lake which had once echoed with the laughter of a dozen brothers and sisters – among them a black-haired, sharp-eyed boy called Eugene.

Less than six weeks after the investiture, and some ten weeks after the fated operation of 12 February, the unforgiving sea returned the body of Eugene Esmonde to the shores of the land he had died defending. On Sunday, 26 April 1942, a body was spotted in the Thames Estuary by the crew of a small boat and was towed in to Sheerness dockyard. Identification was not readily apparent, except that it had been supported in the water by a semi-inflated life-jacket of the type commonly used by air crews. Accordingly, the body was placed on the back of a small truck and driven by an RAF airman from the RAF post at Sheerness, R.V. Mitchell, to the mortuary at the Sheerness RAF unit. The outer sodden garments were removed to reveal the uniform of a Royal Navy Lieutenant-Commander with the gold wire badge of a pilot on the tunic sleeve. Further examination revealed a gold ring on the left little finger, bearing the word 'Jerusalem'.* Enquiries to the Admiralty confirmed that this was the mortal remains of Eugene Esmonde, VC. Official notification of the body's discovery was sent to Eily Esmonde and Eugene's nearest relatives, and a funeral arranged to take place in Gillingham New Cemetery on Thursday, 30 April.

The final interment of Eugene Esmonde was accorded full naval honours. The religious ceremony was presided over by the Roman Catholic chaplain of the nearby naval barracks, the Reverend Father M.B. Egan, while representing the family as mourners were his brothers Owen and Patrick, and sister Carmel with her husband Dermot, an RAF Pilot Officer. Also present were Vice-Admiral Sir George H. D'Oyly Lyon, C-in-C, The Nore, and the Fifth Sea Lord, Rear Admiral A.L. St G. Lyster, CB, CVO, DSO representing the First Sea Lord and the Board of Admiralty respectively, apart from many other senior RN and FAA officers. Civic tribute was accorded by the attendance of the Mayor of Gillingham, Councillor F.R. White, and members of the Corpora-

---

* 'Jerusalem' appears in the Esmonde coat of arms.

Funeral of Eugene Esmonde at Gillingham Cemetery on 30 April 1942.

tion. Over the grave Father Egan said of Esmonde:

'I knew him very well and he never said an uncharitable word of anyone. He was so kind, so good, he was a man in a thousand. He went out like the Crusaders of old for King and Country, and in defence of the religion of his forefathers.'

As the coffin was lowered into the grave an RN firing party fired volley salutes, and as it came to rest a Royal Marine played the traditional bugle calls 'Last Post' and 'Reveille'; the poignant notes echoing across the river which had returned Eugene to his final resting place. Among the many wreaths laid at the graveside was one from the Countess of Limerick, bearing the inscription: 'In honoured memory of a great Irishman'.

When Eugene's will was executed it contained the simple provision that his net estate, £5,020, was to go entirely to his beloved mother Eily: his final acknowledgment of his unwavering devotion to the courageous woman who had given him birth and given her life to her children. Some two years after Eugene's death, Father Wulstan Dobbins, the first Roman Catholic priest to be appointed to the Fleet Air Arm, was appointed to the FAA air base at Lee-on-Solent. Here he arranged for the building of an RC Church, St Michael's, and then enlisted the aid of two RN Captains and several RN Commanders to design a permanent monument to Eugene. The resulting commemoration took the form of a brass plaque mounted on oak, which was placed on the epistle side of the church's altar, adorned on both sides by a pair of finely wrought brass candelabra.

The English rendering of the plaque's Latin inscription reads: 'In pious and perpetual memory of Lt Cdr Eugene Esmonde, RN, VC DSO and all the faithful of the FAA who laid down their lives for their friends in the Great War.'

Though resited within the entrance door of St Michael's now (1983), one result of various church alterations made since 1946, the plaque remains as a permanent reminder of unmatched courage and devotion to duty.

CHAPTER THIRTEEN

Fiasco

We owe respect to the living;
To the dead we owe only truth.
Voltaire, 1785

The events which followed the sacrifice of 825 Squadron FAA on 12 February 1942, though no part of Eugene Esmonde's own life-story, are, nevertheless, directly relevant in the context of the near-chaotic background mismanagement, disorganisation, and in some facets sheer stupidity which characterised *Operation Fuller*, and thereby were in great degree directly responsible for the deaths of Esmonde and almost all his faithful crews. As has already been emphasised in previous chapters, *Fuller* started, and mostly remained, based on a false premise – that should the Brest battleships ever attempt a 'break-out' to German ports via the English Channel, they would leave Brest by day and therefore negotiate the most hazardous section of their journey, i.e. the narrow eastern waters of the Channel, by night.

Thus, when Esmonde *originally* volunteered his squadron for a torpedo attack as part of the plan, he laboured under the impression that his Swordfish crews would at least be able to extract a modicum of 'protection' from the cloak of night. Accordingly, he had part-briefed and trained his crews towards such an operation up until literally the last hour before 825 Squadron actually left Manston to carry out their attack. In the subsequent official inquiry into the actions and failure of *Fuller*, the resulting report re-emphasised this basic aspect by saying; 'The probability that the enemy would pass in the dark hours coloured all the actions of Coastal Command and the Admiralty and influenced arrangements made for patrols, both as to their design and application.'

This bland piece of officialese thinly disguised the simple fact

that all naval and aerial patrol and watchdog forces designated in
Fuller were to be actuated only in daylight hours. Pre-dawn
'readiness' and 'alert' status for air and sea forces were, in effect, to
be stood down to a more leisurely alertness state once daylight
came. Why such a contingency plan should not have given equal
preparation for night operations is, to say the very least, puzzling.
Fuller had been conceived many months before February 1942, and
the normal purpose of any Service contingency planning is to
consider *all* alternatives to the main theme and their possible
'antidotes'.

Yet, as late as 4 February 1942, Rear Admiral Power, the
Assistant Chief of Naval Staff (Home Operations) consulted with
Air Chief Marshal Sir Philip Joubert, AOC-in-C, RAF Coastal
Command, and both concluded that a break-out from Brest was
not only imminent but would come through the English Channel,
and would enter the Dover Straits zone *during darkness*. It was a view
shared by Admiral Bertram Ramsay at Dover, who was of the
opinion that the German ships would probably reach the Straits
'about two hours before dawn'. This consensus of high-ranked
opinion was then passed on by Power to the First Sea Lord, Sir
Dudley Pound at the Admiralty. It was to remain the official view
until 12 February.

The second major failure of the *Fuller* plan was in allocating
sufficiently strong forces to match any break-out force from Brest.
Since the core of *Fuller* was primarily a naval matter, the prime
consideration for countermeasures fell to the Admiralty. At the
beginning of February 1942 the British Home Fleet's main strength
was anchored in Scapa Flow in a watchdog role, to keep a sharp
and ready eye upon the German raider *Tirpitz* which was
harboured in Trondheim, Norway; a semi-chained guard against
any attempt by this battleship to break out of the North Sea via the
northern route into the open Atlantic, where she could prey on
Allied convoys *et al.* The First Sea Lord, Dudley Pound, adamantly
refused to permit any of his Scapa-based heavy ships to be included
in the *Fuller* plan, stating: 'On no account will heavy ships be
brought south where they will be exposed to enemy air attack,
torpedo-boat attack, and risk being damaged by our own or enemy
mine-fields.'

On the face of it, this refusal to commit ships of the Home Fleet with sufficient fire-power and performance to match the German battleships could be interpreted as a failure on the part of Pound to appreciate the needs of the *Fuller* defences. However, the decision must be placed in its contemporary context. The Royal Navy had only recently lost two capital ships, *Repulse* and *Prince of Wales*, off Malaya to Japanese aerial attacks. In the Atlantic were numerous convoys, both to and from the USA and Canada, and conveying essential troop reinforcements to the North African campaign. Pound could hardly be blamed for not wishing to risk an already thinly-stretched remaining Home Fleet to an area which would permit – theoretically – saturation Luftwaffe attacks upon his remaining capital ships; while the reality of existing need for convoy protection had to take priority over any hypothetical contingency measures against an enemy force ostensibly 'contained' for the moment in its own harbours hundreds of miles away. Moreover, if the German ships chose to remain based in Brest, they represented a genuine threat to all Allied shipping crossing the Bay of Biscay, such as troop convoys to Egypt, and were the main elements of the Home Fleet to be stationed as requested by the *Fuller* advocates, i.e. somewhere along the east coast of England, they would be in the wrong location for any countermoves against enemy raiders in Biscay.

Instead a form of 'compromise' was proposed, whereby the Home Fleet 'big girls' remained at Scapa Flow, but Pound ordered six elderly destroyers to Harwich (Dover was not suitable as a destroyer base), in addition to MTBs based at Dover and Ramsgate. The only naval air formation to be included in this force, which in toto came under the operational aegis of Admiral Ramsay at Dover, was 825 Squadron FAA, which was ordered from its normal base at Lee-on-Solent to the forward RAF airfield at Manston. In addition several mine-sweepers were detailed to lay mine fields athwart the exit at the east end of the Channel, these being supplemented by more sea mines being 'sown' by RAF Bomber Command at various stages of the assumed German route.

The inclusion of Esmonde's Swordfish squadron was in fact a 'bonus' thought inspired by Admiral Ramsay. Consultations with ACM Sir Philip Joubert and others had reached a mutual agreement that the most effective weapon which would be used against the German battleships was the airborne torpedo. Accordingly, Joubert had earmarked three of his Bristol Beaufort torpedo-bomber squadrons for *Fuller*, Nos 42, 86, and 217 Squadrons. No 42 Squadron, commanded by Wing Commander M.F.D. Williams, had fourteen Beauforts and was based at Leuchars in Scotland, with a waiting role to attack the *Tirpitz* should she move out from Trondheim. No 86 Squadron, commanded by Wing Commander C.J.P. Flood, was based at St Eval, Cornwall with twelve Beauforts; while 217 Squadron had three Beauforts at St Eval and its other seven aircraft at Thorney Island, just inland from Portsmouth. Leaving Nos 86 and 217 Squadrons where they were, Joubert issued orders for 42 Squadron to fly south to North Coates, near Hull on the east coast.

This geographical spread of torpedo-bombers from Cornwall to Hampshire, Kent, and Lincolnshire appeared to offer excellent opportunities for attacking the German ships at four stages of their projected route. At this stage of planning, however, no concerted attack in full force by any combination of squadrons was mooted – each unit would make an individual attack. Esmonde's Swordfish – the so-termed 'night force' – would attack according to the night conditions. If moonlight was available the Swordfish were to attack as a squadron, but if there was no moonlight each crew would go in individually. Theoretically therefore, Nos 86 and 217 Squadrons' Beauforts would be engaging the enemy ships *before* any need to employ Esmonde's men. The latter would be despatched *if* the ships reached the Dover Straits, while 42 Squadron would complete its part, *if* required, by an attack in the early daylight hours after Esmonde's pre-dawn sortie.

That, at least, was the plan – on paper. In the event the translation from paper to practice proved disastrous, due in part to pure circumstances, but largely to procrastination and delayed execution by Joubert himself and members of his HQ staff. Poor staff work and organisation resulted in a lack of the right equipment in the right place; while the move south by 42 Squadron, originally ordered to take place on 8 February, was delayed for four days due to atrocious weather conditions but also administrative foul-ups. When, on 12 February, the squadron finally left Leuchars it suffered a succession of problems, of which more later, not all of which could be properly attributed to 'natural causes'.

Perhaps the greatest handicap to the air aspects of *Operation Fuller*, nevertheless, was the incredibly tight 'security' blanket thrown over these facets of the plan – a prime example of bureaucracy gone mad which deprived virtually every airman actually flying on 12 February of any clue as to what he was supposed to be doing, or indeed why he was flying at all. This unintentional ignorance was to apply to RAF fighter pilots initially detailed off to escort Esmonde's Swordfish, and to a majority of later sorties undertaken against 'enemy shipping in the Channel'. It also applied to the Beaufort crews eventually despatched, none of whom were told the size or strength or identity of their objectives except in deliberately vague terms. The subsequent official inquiry stated, in part: 'Apart from the weakness of our forces, the main reason for our failure to do more damage to the enemy was the fact that his presence was not detected earlier … '; an indirect barb aimed at the RAF's failure to maintain the Coastal Command *Stopper*, *Habo*, and *Line SE* watchdog patrols, but in reality a veiled criticism of the wireless and R/T silence maintained by Group Captain Victor Beamish when he first sighted the German ships. Though the inquiry report made no direct criticism of Beamish's strict adherence to the general order for W/T and R/T silence during fighter operations, it remains a clear example of the consequences of an inflexible attitude to the contemporary 'security' ruling for *Fuller*. Had Beamish reported his sighting of the ships immediately he might have initiated the *Fuller* plan some 45 minutes before his actual return to base. Add to that the time it took Beamish to get Leigh-Mallory to the telephone, and at least one vital hour was lost; an hour which might have permitted the full fighter escort of five squadrons to have been despatched in ample time to rendezvous with Esmonde's squadron, and may well have made the difference between life and death for Esmonde and his crews.

What remains a mystery is the *apparent* non-receipt of Squadron Leader Oxspring's specific sighting report by any British radio operator – it seems logical that if the German listening service received this message clearly, then so should the British equivalent.

A further consequence of the obsessive concern for security on the part of the RAF was the sorry saga of Coastal Command's small force of Beaufort torpedo-bombers. No 217 Squadron's seven Beauforts at Thorney Island began preparations for take-off shortly before noon on 12 February, when a staff officer at the station telephoned No 11 Group, Fighter Command to request a fighter escort to rendezvous with the Beauforts over Manston at 1.30 pm. In the event three of the seven Beauforts were unserviceable, delaying take-off for the other four until 1.25 pm. By the time this quartet reached Manston their fighter escort had already departed some twenty minutes previously on receiving orders to fly out to sea and attack an 'enemy convoy'.

After circling Manston for some time, the four Beauforts became frustrated, two of them set course out to sea, while the other pair landed at Manston to ask where their escort had got to. No one at Thorney Island had thought to warn 11 Group that the Beauforts would be later arriving than the arranged rendezvous time; nor had any of the Beaufort crews been told the nature of the target – merely that they were to find and attack an 'enemy convoy'. The two Beauforts which landed were quickly briefed as to their true objective, their aircraft were refuelled, and they set off to sea quickly. Meanwhile the three Beauforts left behind at Thorney Island had finally taken off and arrived over Manston, picked up their escorts, and set off. All seven of 217's Beauforts were forced to fight their way through the German fighter screens, filthy weather conditions, and – on reaching their targets – a storm of flak, but none achieved a clear run for their torpedoes, and all suffered extensive damage.

No 42 Squadron's fourteen Beauforts eventually left Leuchars for North Coates, only to be diverted first to Bircham Newton, then finally Coltishall, some six miles north of Norwich. Three of their aircraft were without torpedoes, while Coltishall, being a fighter station, had no technical facilities to service torpedo-bomber aircraft. All fourteen had landed at Coltishall at 11.45 am. Of these, apart from the three unarmed aircraft, two others were declared unserviceable to fly, and the remaining nine did not take-off until 2.16 pm. Reaching Manston at 2.53 pm, the Beauforts met a gaggle of Lockheed Hudsons from No 407 Squadron RCAF over the airfield which were, ostensibly, to lead them to the 'enemy convoy' and help in the attack by 'diversionary' bombing of the ships. Again, due to inadequate and garbled briefings, the two formations continued to circle Manston, each seeming to assume that the other was the leader.

This farcical situation was eventually resolved when Squadron Leader W.H. Cliff of 42 Squadron decided to end the nonsense and led his Beauforts out over the North Sea, followed by six of the eleven Hudsons. Soon after the Hudsons lost contact with Cliff due to the appalling weather conditions, but found part of the German destroyer and E-boat force which they bombed, losing two Hudsons in the process. Finally arriving over the German ships, Cliff and his men arrived as several British destroyers were engaged in close combat with enemy force. Dropping to sea level, Cliff led his Beaufort crews in to a series of individual attacks, though one Beaufort mistook the British destroyer *Campbell* for an enemy and tried to torpedo it. None of the 'tin fish' found their mark on the German battleships.

The third of Joubert's Beaufort units, No 86 Squadron at St Eval, flew its twelve aircraft to Thorney Island, arriving there at 2.30 pm and being sent on to Coltishall. Again, Coltishall had no torpedoes for the unarmed Beauforts, so they returned to Thorney Island to be armed up, then flew to Manston, reaching this airfield at 5 pm. Here they were told the latest known location of the enemy ships and set off, reaching the briefed location by 5.41 pm. By that time the German naval formation was some 50 miles further north-east. While searching vainly for the German 'convoy' the Beauforts spotted four mine-sweepers and attacked these. Two Beauforts failed to return. Thus, the sum total of Coastal Command's contribution to the day's attacks had been twenty-eight Beauforts and eleven Hudsons in unco-ordinated sorties, none of which had achieved any positive success, and most of which had suffered varying degrees of damage and crew casualties from the German defences *et al.*

None of the crews had been properly briefed as to their actual targets, while the administrative and technical 'back-up' had been almost wholly inefficient or completely lacking. The frustration and

anger felt by most Beaufort crews afterwards were probably
succinctly summed up in the words of Squadron Leader Cliff when,
on telephoning a Group Captain to report, he exploded: 'I was sent
looking for a convoy. Why was I not told about the bloody great
battleships!!?'

Bomber Command's part in the operations of 12 February was in
most ways merely an extension of the general unpreparedness and
hasty improvisation exemplified in every other aerial facet of *Fuller*.
In the initial planning, the Command agreed to 'reserve' a force of
300 bombers for *Fuller* at a state of two hours' 'Readiness', bombed
up with pre-briefed crews on immediate standby. The Command
operational order for this arrangement, dated 1 May 1941,
specified among other conditions:

> The ships will be attacked by surface craft and aircraft by day. It
> is not intended that aircraft (bombers) should attack by night.
> Unless suitable cloud cover is available, attacks will not be
> ordered except in areas where Fighter Command can give
> protection. It is unlikely that the enemy will pass the Straits of
> Dover in daylight.

The AOC-in-C, Bomber Command then was Air Marshal Sir
Richard Peirse who, by February 1942, was concerned by the large
proportion of his Command's offensive strength – almost 40 per
cent of establishment, but nearer 70 per cent of actual aircraft with
crews available – being 'set aside' for a hypothetical situation.
Accordingly, on 6 February, he requested the Air Ministry to
release him from the *Fuller* obligation, only to be told to consult the
Admiralty. Understandably the Admiralty demurred, pointing out
that the need for *Fuller* was now becoming vital. Peirse then, on his
own responsibility and *without informing the Admiralty*, quietly
reduced the standby force from 300 to 100 bombers and crews, and
reduced their 'Readiness' state to four hours' notification, with only
50 per cent of aircraft actually bombed up at any given time. A few
days later, however, Peirse amended the latter order to having all
100 bombers loaded at all times. Meantime he supplied a few
bombers for mine-laying operations off the Frisians – a form of
naval-air co-operation which the Command had been carrying out

since the start of the war.

At 11.40 am on 12 February Peirse's headquarters received formal notification that the Brest battleships were nearing the Dover Straits; followed at 12.32 pm by an Air Ministry signal (addressed to Bomber, Fighter, and Coastal Commands) which demanded; 'Maximum forces to be employed as early as possible to destroy enemy ships and aircraft. This unique opportunity to be exploited to the utmost.'

This created an immediate problem in Bomber Command. Even including the 100 aircraft 'allotted' already to stand-by for *Fuller*, the Command could barely muster 240 aircraft and crews in a fit state for immediate operations. Of these the 100 stand-by bombers were already bombed-up – but with the wrong types of bomb for low altitude attacks in the cloudy conditions of that day. The other aircraft had to be bombed up, fuelled, and their crews gathered in, briefed, and prepared. While this meant frantic activity at all operational bomber stations, it also meant that the first Bomber Command sorties against the ships could not be mounted much before 2.30 pm, and indeed the first 'wave' comprising seventy-three bombers drawn from various stations did not begin to get airborne until 2.20 pm, with the first arriving over the target area shortly before 3 pm. Eventually three more 'waves' were to leave, the last at 6.15 pm. All attacks were carried out in piecemeal fashion, often by individual aircraft – no concerted bombing was possible. Of an overall total of 242 bombers despatched, only thirty-nine reported sighting and/or attacking enemy ships. Of these fifteen failed to return, while another crashed badly on return to base. In retrospect it is difficult to see how the bombers could have achieved any real success. In early 1942 RAF Bomber Command had yet to perfect the art of precision bombing i.e. hitting a specific target. Radar navigation and bombing aids were yet to be generally fitted to the aircraft, while the crews had little or no practical experience of attempting to bomb a moving target such as a ship travelling at 25-30 knots.

While Bomber and Coastal Commands had their parts in the operations, the most significant Command in the context of Esmonde's squadron attack was Fighter; in particular the fighters of Leigh-Mallory's No 11 Group. On the morning of 12 February the Group strength comprised twenty-five Spitfire and Hurricane squadrons, or a total of some 500-plus serviceable, operationally-ready aircraft with pilots. In the *Fuller* context No 11 Group was responsible primarily for providing fighter escorts, when required, to Bomber and Coastal Command sorties, with additional roles of *Jim Crow* reconnaissance flights over the Channel, and possible fighter-bomber operations against surface shipping. While maintaining a daily proportion of its fighters on 'readiness' state prior to dawn, the Group would normally remain on the *qui vive* generally, awaiting specific requests for particular escorts from the other two Commands. Despite its very nature as a prime offensive weapon, requiring instant reaction to any emergency, and a flexible response; No 11 Group administration, control, and policy reflected to some degree the tight influence of its commander, Trafford Leigh-Mallory.

A career officer of undisguised ambitious bent, Leigh-Mallory was an example of the long-serving staff officer to whom routine, unruffled by sudden decisions, was the epitome of good Service procedure. In character too he was very much aloof from anyone of subordinate rank, seldom able to mix freely and easily with the men he commanded. It was therefore natural for Leigh-Mallory to gather around him at HQ staff level a number of officers of similar outlook to some degree; men who would seldom, if ever, contradict him or oppose his views and policies. Even so, Leigh-Mallory remained to a great degree isolated from his juniors in rank, gaining a reputation among these as virtually unapproachable, and intolerant of interference or opposition. In the hallowed walls of a staff college or Air Ministry office such qualities as Leigh-Mallory possessed would have contributed much to the smooth running of the never-ending sifting of paperwork which constitutes 'staff administration' – in the driving seat of a firstline, fighting spearhead force such qualities are seldom the prime requirements.

It is therefore readily understandable that Leigh-Mallory's character imposed itself firmly upon the attitudes of many of his staff and subordinates, frowning heavily on any examples of individual officers in posts of reasonable authority status displaying personal initiative in any moment of crisis. Naturally, there were several exceptions to this generalisation – the independent attempts by Squadron Leader Bill Igoe to alert 11 Group HQ to the presence of the German battleships in the Channel, and his subsequent actions, stand out as a prime example of such 'rebels' against the pervading attitudes at Group Headquarters. As stated previously, Igoe's initial attempts to initiate the *Fuller* plan early in the morning of 12 February met with lack-lustre interest at 11 Group HQ, thereby forfeiting precious time. While it is true that part-blame for this lack of interest at HQ level at first was due to the secrecy imposed upon the whole plan – thus most HQ staff knew little or nothing of the meaning of the code-word *Fuller* – nevertheless, any staff officer accustomed to exercising fully his own initiative and authority might reasonably have been expected to react more intelligently to Igoe's original warning. The relatively lethargic responses received from 11 Group HQ by several men vitally concerned with *Fuller* – particularly Flight Lieutenant Gerald Kidd at Swingate, and Wing Commander Constable-Roberts at Admiral Ramsay's headquarters – was singled out for mention in the otherwise extraordinary bland report of the subsequent official inquiry:

> Unfortunately, No 11 Group, who were responsible for the *Jim Crow* reconnaissance, were not sufficiently alive to the fact that the German ships might be coming out about that time. True, they knew that *Operation Fuller* was in operation but some of the witnesses said they had not been informed that there had been any breakdown in the night patrols, and in consequence their minds were not especially directed to the possible significance of the radar plots;* and they were slow to order investigation by additional reconnaissance. Had these plots been investigated as soon as their character came under suspicion, it is possible that the enemy squadron would have been sighted an appreciable time earlier than it was.

The general inefficiency at Group HQ level undoubtedly con-tributed primarily to the 'loss' of some two hours to the eventual initiation of the *Fuller* plan, and was part exacerbated by the

---

* This, in spite of Igoe's initial warning ... Author.

reluctance – in one case, blank refusal – by any of Leigh-Mallory's staff officers to disturb their master during his ceremonial duties at Northolt when requested to do so, first by Squadron Leader Bobby Oxspring, then later Group Captain Victor Beamish. A more direct consequence of that inefficiency was the failure to fulfil Group's promise of adequate fighter escorts for Eugene Esmonde's 825 Squadron – a failure which must bear a large part of the ultimate responsibility for permitting Esmonde and his men to undertake what can only be described as a suicidal sortie. If such condemnation appears harsh, then the following facts should be considered.

Flight Lieutenant Gerald Kidd at Swingate had the immediate responsibility for 'controlling' Esmonde's squadron on operations while it was based at Manston, and was immediately answerable to Wing Commander Constable-Roberts at Dover for this responsibility. Constable-Roberts, in turn, was Admiral Ramsay's air liaison officer and thus the 'authority' for any decision by Ramsay to permit 825 Squadron to attack the German battleships, or not. Once Esmonde and his men had taken off from Manston, under the distinct impression that they were to rendezvous with and thereafter be protected by five squadrons of fighters, Kidd attempted to keep in touch with both the Swordfish and the promised fighters. He was informed by Manston that the Swordfish had indeed taken off and were circling the airfield, while the Hornchurch control assured Kidd that their fighters were also over Manston at that time. Rechecking with Manston, Kidd was disturbed to hear that there were in fact no fighters over Manston as yet. Kidd promptly telephoned Hornchurch again and asked the female operator there to put him in touch with the Controller again, only to be told that he was busy at the plotting table. Kidd persisted, telling the woman to check with the Controller as to where precisely the Swordfish were. Her reply was that the Controller 'didn't know'. Kidd refused to accept this and insisted that the Controller check his radar plots for precise location of the Swordfish. Only then did the Controller at Hornchurch tell Kidd that the promised fighter escort had yet to join up with Esmonde's Swordfish.

This statement left Gerald Kidd thoroughly dismayed, then

angry. Had Hornchurch told him in the first place that the fighters might or even would be late for the arranged rendezvous time, Kidd could, indeed, would have prevented Esmonde taking off. His view was echoed by Constable-Roberts and Bertram Ramsay; the latter having authorised Esmonde to leave on the sole condition that the fighters *would* be provided on time, as promised by 11 Group. By the time all three men were fully aware of 11 Group's failure, Esmonde was dying and 12 of his men were either already dead or about to die ...

The national outrage at the (apparently) unscathed German battleships actually sailing within gun range of England's southern coast and escaping destruction erupted from the day following the 'Channel Dash' operations. The cost of the operations on the British side had been six Swordfish, seventeen fighters, and at least twenty bombers, apart from naval casualties aboard surface craft involved; a total of almost 100 airmen and sailors killed and dozens of others seriously wounded or injured. On the German side the losses amounted to merely seventeen aircraft, eleven airmen and thirteen seamen killed, and sixty-eight seamen suffered varying degrees of injury.

Winston Churchill, the Prime Minister, faced a storm of protest and anger in the House of Commons and was forced to set up an immediate official inquiry board to investigate and report on this disastrous reverse in Allied fortune. Presided over by Mr Justice Bucknill, its two other members were Vice-Admiral Sir Hugh Binney for the Admiralty and Air Chief Marshal Sir Edgar Ludlow-Hewitt, Inspector-General, RAF. These met on Monday, 16 February and sat for fifteen days. The board had no authority to compel any admirals to attend, but its members heard 'evidence' from many naval and air officers, many of whom used the occasion simply to 'justify' their own failures in the matter.

It quickly became apparent to many individuals attending the inquiry that many truths were not going to be aired or considered, and the board seemed to be doing nothing more than whitewash the whole miserable affair in the interests of restoring confidence in Churchill's government and the most senior Service chiefs. When, for example, Squadron Leader Bill Igoe attended the board in Whitehall he was approached by an official and asked what

Avro Manchester L7477, QR-N of 61 Sqn at Woolfox Lodge, displaying some of its flak scars after the 'Channel Dash' operation.

evidence he proposed to give. In Igoe's words:

'I said, the truth, and when I reached the stand I was asked if I had heard the previous officer's evidence, which was unconnected with mine, and if I disagreed with anything in it. I replied that I found it accurate – we were then both discharged without further consideration, without me being questioned at all, so that my evidence was never heard.'

Flight Lieutenant Gerald Kidd, who had submitted a lengthy and scathing report to the Air Ministry (which was read by Churchill later), gave evidence to the inquiry board, then had lunch with Admiral Ramsay at the Senior Services Club, where Ramsay told him: 'It's a waste of time. You might as well turn round and go home. They're not even taking notes – all they want is a whitewash.' Bertram Ramsay was one of the very few senior officers involved in *Fuller* to be completely honest and objective about his own failure to anticipate the German arrival off Dover accurately, and his only criticism of any other participants was his bitter regrets at the failure of RAF Fighter Command to get its promised escort to Eugene Esmonde on time. His objectivity was not particularly matched among several other senior officers, who tended to try shifting blame and responsibility for errors in judgment or execution onto the shoulders of other Service chiefs.

Ramsay's official report was also honest and to the point in indicating the errors and omissions in the execution of the *Fuller* plan, with particular criticism of the parts played by RAF Fighter, Coastal and Bomber Commands; this criticism being wholly supported by the reports of his RAF liaison officers. Ramsay's report received no mention in the subsequently *published* records of the board's findings. It was by no means the only evidence to be submerged under a deep sea of 'security' waves.

At RAF Biggin Hill Flight Lieutenant Cowan Douglas-Stephenson had always kept a personal daily log of every possible event of interest to happen on the airfield throughout his first tour of duty there, which included 12 February 1942. Shortly after he was posted to Hornchurch, but on returning to Biggin Hill some time later he browsed through his log – only to find the pages from 3 January to 25 March 1942 had been neatly removed with a razor blade. Yet every other entry he had ever made was still intact.

Though this minor vandalism might well have been the work of some 'souvenir-hunter', Douglas-Stephenson himself was convinced it was a deliberate attempt to 'lose' his detailed record of the events of 12 February.

The Bucknill Report (Command Paper 6775) reached Churchill first in early March 1942, and on 18 March the Deputy Prime Minister, Clement Attlee, produced it in Parliament. Attlee made it plain to the Members that, 'in the interest of national security', its contents would not be made public. On the same pretext Attlee (and Churchill later) gave few details in reply to the many questions raised by the Members. Attlee then concluded by saying, 'The general findings do not reveal that there were any serious deficiencies in foresight, co-operation, or organisation between the Services concerned and their respective Commands' – a statement so blatantly astonishing to the MPs at the time that it merely provoked fury on the benches, and did nothing to abate the continuing demand by the public Press for the truth.

Nevertheless, the Bucknill Report remained secret and unpublished until 1946. Even then the published version patently contained many omissions, and failed to provide answers to many vital questions. In a broader, objective view, the findings of the inquiry board must be placed against the events of that period of the war. On almost every fighting front until 1942 the Allies had suffered defeat after defeat, with few successes to bolster Allied morale. Then, on 15 February 1942 – just three days after the Channel Dash fiasco – the 'impregnable fortress' of Singapore surrendered to invading Japanese forces. At such a moment the need for unity in purpose and determination among the Allies, especially the British population and its Empire partners, was paramount in the view of Churchill and his government. To have pursued an in-depth witch-hunt into the failure of *Operation Fuller*, naming 'culprits' and allotting official blame *publicly*, could only have added unnecessary misery to existing misery about the conduct of the war by contemporary Service and political leaders.

This is not to say that heads did not roll, and a number of officers known to have expressed blunt criticism of the way that *Fuller* had been executed, or had openly declared the Bucknill inquiry's findings to be whitewash, were quietly shuffled into backwater postings, far removed from 'sharp end' operations; men like Wing Commander Constable-Roberts who suddenly found himself transferred from Dover and posted to Scapa Flow. Before the end of the year Sir Philip Joubert was succeeded in his post as AOC-in-C, Coastal Command and moved to the Far East, though having been in that post since June 1941 and not actually leaving it until February 1943, it may have been merely a normal 'end-of-tour' posting. At the other end of the scale of reactions, a sprinkling of awards and decorations were promulgated in March 1942 for various RAF and RN personnel who had particularly distinguished themselves during the actions on 12 February. On 28 March, however, one of the principal figures of controversy in the 'Channel Dash' affair, Group Captain Victor Beamish, set out in a Spitfire from Kenley towards Calais – and never returned, having been shot down during a skirmish with German fighters over the Channel.

If the German navy achieved a moral and tactical victory on 12 February 1942, it was also a strategical blunder in the long view. The *Gneisenau*, *Scharnhorst*, and *Prinz Eugen* reached their German destinations with only damage caused by striking sea mines during the last stages of their journey. *Gneisenau*'s damage put her into Kiel dry dock for repairs where, only two weeks later, RAF bombers caught her and severely damaged her. She was later towed to Gdynia and became a harbour defence blockship. *Scharnhorst*, which had also hit a mine en route, was repaired and in February 1943 joined *Tirpitz* in Norway. On 6 September that year she joined with *Tirpitz* in bombarding Allied wireless installations on the island of Spitzbergen but her next intended foray, to attack a British convoy heading for Russia at Christmas 1943, proved fatal. On 26 December *Scharnhorst*, only one day out of port, was trapped by the British Home Fleet off North Cape. Continuous gun and torpedo attacks finally sank her at 7.45 pm when the giant ship died in a horrendous explosion. Of her crew of 1,940 only 36 men survived – all of them non-commissioned seamen. *Prinz Eugen*, last of the trio, made several abortive attempts to 'rejoin' the war, but in the event took no active part in operations and survived the war to become an American trials ship for the initial hydrogen bomb tests, during which she was sunk.

Thus, the three ships' much acclaimed (in Germany) dash

through the English Channel proved to be effectively their swan-song in the context of the naval war. Hitler's concentration of the German navy's capital ships within the North Sea zone suited the British Admiralty well. As Winston Churchill explained in a letter to Franklin Roosevelt, President of the USA:

> The naval situation in home waters and in the Atlantic has been definitely eased by the retreat [*sic*] of the naval forces from Brest. From there they threatened all our eastbound convoys enforcing a constant two-battleship escort. Our bomber effort can now be concentrated on Germany.

His final comment here reflected the RAF's relief at being now able to diminish the strength and urgency of Bomber Command's protracted aerial campaign against the 'Ugly Sisters'* at Brest, and therefore strengthen its nightly offensive over the Reich.

The long-term effects of *Operation Cerebus* had certainly not been lost in the minds of many senior German naval officers. As Grand-Admiral Raeder, supremo of the German navy expressed it; 'It was a tactical success but a strategic defeat'. In his report Raeder also made plain his view that the move of his ships from Brest had not been necessary if only the Luftwaffe had supplied an adequate air umbrella protection for the port. For the Luftwaffe's reluctance to make such provision Raeder blamed directly Hermann Göring, the overall commander of the air forces, saying: 'He therefore robbed us of a chance to do something worthwhile in convoy raiding.' Despite such reservations by the naval hierarchy, the German nation greeted the news of the operation with huge delight – a much-needed fillip to national morale in the light of the depressing situation along the Russian front at that period.

Adolf Galland, who had masterminded and controlled *Operation Thunderbolt*, the Luftwaffe's successful part in the overall operation, was in no doubt of its achievement, saying: 'Objectively speaking, the break-through by the group of battle-cruisers with their escort vessels under the air umbrella of the German fighters constitutes, in

---

* The RAF's common nickname for *Scharnhorst* and *Gneisenau*; another soubriquet being 'Salmon and Gluckstein'.

Reunion. L-R: 'Pat' Kingsmill; Edgar Lee; and Donald Bunce relive memories in a Fairey Swordfish at Lee-on-Solent, 1967.

planning and execution, a great and impressive victory ... the co-operation between the German naval and air forces was exemplary, both in preparation and execution of the operation.'

His personal tribute to the Allied airmen was both incisive and perceptive: 'The pilots of the RAF fought bravely, tenaciously and untiringly, but had been sent into action with insufficient planning, without a clear concept of the attack, without a centre of gravity and without systematic tactics.'*

When, on 12 January 1942, Adolf Hitler had set his personal seal on the decision to move the Brest group of ships, he had remarked: 'I do not believe the British capable of making and carrying out lightning decisions.' In the matter under discussion then his much-trumpeted 'intuition' proved entirely accurate. Yet even Hitler would probably have been astonished that the British reaction was to be so unco-ordinated and so hastily improvised, and then made in such piecemeal fashion. Nor would he have believed that even

* *The First and The Last*; Methuen, 1955

with some ten months' pre-planning for just such an operation, any nation with Britain's proud military and naval history should allot defensive forces inadequate in overall fighting strength; an appreciation shared by the members of the Bucknill board of inquiry which referred in its final report to the 'weakness of our forces'.

Perhaps that 'weakness' was due not only to bad planning, but also to a complacent, even smug presumption by (primarily) the Admiralty. With its centuries-old traditions of mastery of the oceans, and the national conceit that termed in every schoolboy's geography book the strip of water along Britain's southern coastline as the 'English Channel'; the thought that *any* 'foreigner' would even contemplate an 'invasion' of those waters seemed a pipe-dream. If indeed such an attitude lingered in the minds of those who originated the planning of *Operation Fuller*, it would in part explain the Assistant Chief of Naval Staff's conception as; 'A simple battle – all forces should be thrown into action at the earliest possible time.'

That 'simple' battle proved to be a blow to British national pride, and resounded around the world – never again could Britain regard 'its' Channel as its greatest defence against foreign invasion. Louis Blériot's cross-Channel aerial hop on 25 July 1909 from France to Dover had been the first omen; the Brest battleships, as they sailed with near-impunity past Dover nearly thirty-three years later, confirmed England's vulnerability.

Epilogue

Despite the storm of scathing criticism of virtually every other facet of *Operation Fuller* which erupted immediately after 12 February, and continued to 'rumble' in subsequent years; the actions of Eugene Esmonde and his crews on that fateful February day have remained universally acclaimed as the epitome of courage, determination, and selfless 'devotion to duty'. No 825 Squadron's superb gallantry shone like a beacon in an otherwise gloomy vista, untarnished by any later account or investigation. Yet there remains one vital question in many minds – why did Eugene Esmonde, though fully aware of the hair-thin chances of survival against such terrifying odds, decide to fly the sortie? He was at no stage actually ordered to do so. Having originally volunteered his squadron to participate in the *Fuller* plan, under given circumstances which no longer applied on the morning of 12 February, he could have demurred from leading his semi-trained crews on what had all the elements of a near-suicide sortie. Had he so refused no stain could be placed on his character or Service record; as a pure volunteer he had the right to refrain had he so wished. That 'right' is evident from the reaction of Admiral Ramsay who had made it quite plain via Wing Commander Constable-Roberts that the final decision was entirely up to Esmonde.

It might be said that, being a regular-serving Royal Navy officer, Esmonde really had no choice in the matter; how can any Serviceman refuse to 'do his duty'? But Ramsay had meant precisely what he had said – only Esmonde *should* decide. This question could only have been answered properly by Eugene Esmonde himself had he survived. Yet at least part of the answer might be derived from the character of the man. Foremost therein was his religious faith in Roman Catholicism, an unwavering belief inherited from his ancestry in which he had been inculcated from his extreme youth, and which had sustained him throughout his life. This faith included high ideals of duty and honour, an unquestionable personal code of behaviour and attitude to his fellow man. This faith gave Esmonde complete confidence in his own abilities without any hint of mere conceit; that self-confidence exemplified by a perfectionist who sets out to master any needed skill and can only achieve a goal by applying himself wholly towards it. Yet Esmonde never expected such high standards in all other men. As a realist he recognised human failings only too well, and therefore made reasonable allowance for any frailties. When dealing with subordinates Esmonde contented himself with issuing necessary orders, giving a clear direction for them to be followed, then in a sense 'stepped back' to let his men carry out his orders, trusting them to live up to their individual responsibilities. Though always maintaining the dignity and status of a commander, he seldom 'interfered' with methods used by subordinates in carrying out orders.

As a leader Eugene Esmonde did not fit the stereotyped image. A fellow officer aboard *Furious* who served alongside Esmonde for almost a year has said of him; 'I could not imagine him leading any forlorn hope. He was one with no great sporting talent in ball games – such as might lead to a form of hero-worship by others not so gifted. Nor was he one of those extrovert theatrical personalities who might have attracted people to him by that awful word "charisma". Nor did he at any time become one of those men described loosely as "born leaders". Again, strangely perhaps, nor was he what I might term a "man-manager". I believe his strength lay actually in pure character, without at all being obvious, coupled with his tremendous professional expertise. I think he could aptly have been described as – as far as naval or any other form of flying was concerned – the "great professional", thus inspiring so much confidence in those that flew under his command.'

His view of Esmonde's professional abilities were echoed by several other men who flew under his command at varying periods. Hugh Hearn, who flew as Esmonde's No 2 in 825 Squadron at one time, said: 'He was a superb pilot and in a very short time taught us all a great deal in operational conditions by his own example.' Yet another pilot, who joined 825 Squadron as a very raw Sub-

Lieutenant pilot aboard *Victorious* shortly before the *Bismarck* operations, recalled Esmonde as:

'Outstanding in not at all an obvious way. He had his priorities right, unfussy, rather scruffy and found time in the middle of a fairly hectic flying programme to welcome me into the squadron. He was a most unusual man – perhaps only his rather rare species – Irish, Catholic, *and* 'upper class' (for want of a better word) – could have produced him. His courage and humour were in no sense a pose, or a remedy for other insecurities, but seemed effortless and utterly predictable. Most of my wartime acquaintances have become 'lost' in a sort of mist – yet with him I experience instant recall, such was the impression he made on me.'

As one of the men who followed behind Esmonde on 12 February 1942, Reginald 'Mac' Samples' memory of his commanding officer is even more significant: 'He was a man of few words whose method of operation seemed to assume that his officers were competent and mature men, and that his role as leader should be confined to setting an example, and not cramping anyone's style by "over-organisation". He was clearly a most experienced airman, but one would never have known this, or indeed anything about his accomplishments, from him. He was modest to a degree, and one's loyalty to him was engendered by his skilled airmanship and his quiet but compulsive personality.'

In Samples', and others', emphasis on Eugene Esmonde's professional skills might lay the main reason that men followed Esmonde so willingly into otherwise fraught situations. A fighting leader's personal example in such matters means far more to his subordinates than mere rank seniority or any other facet of command. In the words of Air Chief Marshal Sir Basil Embry, one of the RAF's most outstanding leaders ever: 'True leadership of any fighting formation could not be conducted with complete success from an office chair, but must spring from physical leadership in the air by the commander.'

In war men do not lightly place their lives in the hands of any man merely because that man holds higher rank on his tunic sleeve – they must believe that their leader *knows* what lays ahead, and can inspire confidence purely by his personal example.

If personal honour and the need for example in leadership were vital aspects of Esmonde's decision to fly his ultimate sortie, then his sense of duty was equally important to him. Duty, to Eugene Esmonde, was implicit with the self-discipline taught by his Catholic faith, and was merely re-emphasised by his regard for Service discipline. His was not a devious character, and ulterior motivation never coloured any decision made. To Esmonde it was a simple matter of accepting fully the responsibility of his rank and position, and obeying orders; not mindlessly but with sincerity and personal conviction. As with all regular-serving professional Servicemen, Esmonde recognised the need for sacrifice in many things in deference to the requirements of his profession; even the unbidden yet ultimate self-sacrifice should this be necessary to furthering the cause of his duty to the Service. Thus, when the moment came for Eugene to give his decision there must have seemed to him no real alternative; his utter dedication to the cause for which the Allies were fighting surmounted any selfish fears or considerations. Some have argued that his decision to fly that day amounted to a form of obstinacy, even stupidity, rather than rational reasoning. But who is really to know or even understand what thoughts must have flickered through Esmonde's brain in the seconds before he irretrievably committed himself and his crews?

In the words of a naval forebear, Lord Howe, 'Some occasions in our profession will justify, if not require, more hazard to be ventured than can systematically be defended by experience.' To Esmonde this was clearly one of those occasions. As has been related, men close to Esmonde at that fateful moment plainly saw the inner torment reflected on his face; the conflict between conscience, faith, and his conception of his sworn duty. Perhaps W.B. Yeats' words in his *An Irish Airman foresees his Death* summed Eugene Esmonde's decision:

> I balanced all, brought all to mind,
> The years to come seemed waste of breath,
> A waste of breath the years behind
> In balance with this life, this death.

Appendixes

Crews & Aircraft,
825 Squadron, FAA,
12 February 1942

Swordfish

1st Sub-Flight:

W5984, 'H'	Lt-Cdr Eugene Esmonde, DSO	*Pilot*
	Lt William Henry Williams	*Observer*
	L/A William John Clinton	*TAG*

W5907, 'L'	Sub-Lt Charles Major Kingsmill	*Pilot*
	Sub-Lt Reginald McCartney Samples	*Observer*
	L/A Donald Arthur Bunce	*TAG*

W5983, 'G'	Sub-Lt Brian Westland Rose	*Pilot*
	Sub-Lt Edgar Frederick Lee	*Observer*
	L/A Ambrose Laurence Johnson, DSM	*TAG*

2nd Sub-Flight:

W4523, 'F'	Lt John Chute Thompson	*Pilot*
	Sub-Lt Robert Laurens Parkinson	*Observer*
	L/A Ernest Topping	*TAG*

W5985, 'K'	Sub-Lt Cecil Ralph Wood	*Pilot*
	Sub-Lt Eric Herbert Fuller-Wright	*Observer*
	L/A Henry Thomas Albert Wheeler	*TAG*

W5978, 'M'	Sub-Lt Peter Bligh	*Pilot*
	Sub-Lt William Beynon	*Observer*
	L/A William Grenville Smith	*TAG*

Fighter Command Intelligence Summary No 312

Operations against an enemy naval force in the Straits of Dover

1. At 1042 hours on 12th February 1942, two Spitfire Vbs on Channel reconnaissance sighted an enemy naval force, believed to comprise the battle cruisers *Scharnhorst* and *Gneisenau*, the cruiser *Prinz Eugen*, three destroyers, and twelve 'E' boats, steaming north-east off Le Treport. They attacked one of the 'E' boats and left it sinking. Between 0800 and 0900 hours on the same morning about six enemy aircraft had operated between Torquay and Portland and had made attacks on the aerodromes at Exeter and Warmwell, possibly as a diversion to cover the movement of the enemy force from Brest.

Thereafter the sequence of events was as follows:

2. Between 1218 and 1225 hours five squadrons of Spitfire Vbs left to escort and support six naval Swordfish detailed to attack the enemy force. Four of the fighter squadrons failed to make rendez-vous, but patrolled the Straits. Pilots of the escort squadron, however, report strikes on the ships, which they attributed to torpedoes. All six Swordfish failed to return, but five members of the crews had been rescued and two bodies have been recovered. Three e/a were destroyed, two probably destroyed, and nine damaged for the loss of one Spitfire and its pilot.

3. From 1230 hours onwards a further three squadrons of Spitfire Vbs patrolled the Straits to provide additional withdrawal cover.

4. At 1240 hours 10 Hurricane bombers IIB left to attack the enemy escort vessels. They were unable to locate their target, but attacked four trawlers or minesweepers off Boulogne. All four vessels are claimed as probably damaged. One Hurricane and its pilot failed to return.

5. Between 1310 and 1340 hours 10 Whirlwinds were despatched to escort destroyers. They failed to sight the destroyers. Four of the Whirlwinds and their pilots failed to return.

6. At 1315 hours 8 Hurricane IIC and 12 Spitfire VBs left to make a low-level attack on the enemy destroyers. Cannon strikes were seen, but otherwise the results of this attack were not observed.

7. At 1320 hours three squadrons of Spitfire VBs left to escort 7 Beauforts of Coastal Command. Rendezvous between the Beauforts and the Spitfires was not made, but six of the Beauforts made torpedo attacks on the warships and claim at least one hit on a battle cruiser. One Beaufort shot down by an Me 109 and one is missing. The Spitfires attacked independently and claim one 'E' boat damaged.

8. Between 1340 and 1355 hours a squadron of Hurricane IIC and a squadron of Spitfires VB left to attack 'E' boats. Nine corvettes or destroyers were attacked and hits were claimed on all of them.

9. Between 1402 and 1440 hours 8 squadrons of Spitfires VB left to maintain air superiority over the target while attacks were delivered by aircraft of Bomber and Coastal Commands. These attacks were delivered as follows:

(i) Two out of nine Hudsons of Coastal Command despatched, attacked merchant vessels and a third a destroyer. In one case the bombs failed to release and in the other two results were not observed. Three Hudsons made no attack, two are missing, and one report has not yet been received.

(ii) A second formation of five Hudsons of Coastal Command failed to meet their escort and returned.

(iii) Out of the first wave of 73 aircraft of Bomber Command, consisting of 35 Wellingtons, 19 Blenheims, 11 Hampdens, 2 Manchesters, and 6 Bostons, 13 aircraft attacked the target, one attacked a target at the Hook of Holland, and another a destroyer. Results generally were not observed.

(iv) Eight out of nine Beauforts of Coastal Command made torpedo attacks and one aircraft reported seeing a warship listing badly and with smoke pouring from the bow. In general, results were not observed.

(v) A second wave of 129 aircraft of Bomber Command, consisting of 52 Hampdens, 41 Wellingtons, 13 Manchesters, 12 Blenheims, 5 Halifaxes, 4 Bostons, and 2 Stirlings, left at 1437 hours. Fifteen aircraft attacked the primary target, and one Stirling reported seeing bursts 150 yards to starboard of a battle cruiser after bombing from 1,500 feet. Seven Hampdens and 2 Wellingtons failed to return, and one Wellington claims an Me.110 probably destroyed.

10. While the above attacks were in progress 8 Hurricane bombers IIC escorted and covered by 8 Hurricanes II and 11 Spitfires VB left to attack 'E' boats and destroyers. In spite of heavy fighter opposition they reached the target and claim one 600-ton vessel bombed and sunk and one of 400 tons damaged.

11. At 1445 hours three squadrons of Spitfires VB left to maintain air superiority over the target and were followed at 1505/1524 hours by a further 40 Spitfires. During this period further attacks by aircraft of Coastal and Bomber Commands were delivered as follows:

(i) At 1600 hours 11 Beauforts of Coastal Command were despatched. One aircraft attacked a destroyer but the torpedo failed to release. Five made no attack and 5 reports are still outstanding.

(ii) At 1615 hours a third wave of 41 bombers, consisting of 19 Wellingtons, 8 Stirlings, 8 Halifaxes, and 6 Blenheims were despatched. Three Blenheims scored possible hits from 11,000 feet and 2 Wellingtons also attacked, but did not observe results. Two Wellingtons are missing.

12. Meanwhile, at 1542 hours, five of our destroyers, operating in two sections, had made contact with the enemy. The first section fired all their torpedoes. Stormy conditions prevented the observation of results, but three loud explosions were heard. The second section fired all their torpedoes at a range of 3,500 yards. Results were not observed, but it is believed that probably one and possibly two hits were scored on the leading cruiser. One of our destroyers was damaged, but has reached port. Five or six more destroyers stood by, but did not fire.

13. Between 1526 and 1722 hours a further 35 Spitfires VB were despatched to patrol the eastern approaches to the Straits of Dover

and cover the withdrawal of our attacking aircraft. At 1630 hours 2 Beaufighters of Coastal Command left to shadow the enemy force. One of them sighted the *Scharnhorst* and 6 destroyers at 1800 hours, about 15 miles south-west of Dan Helder. During the night 2 Catalinas, one Whitley, and one Wellington continued the shadowing process.

14. Altogether in these operations 243 bombers, 41 Coastal Command aircraft, 6 Naval Swordfish, 18 Hurricane bombers, and 323 fighters were despatched. Poor visibility and low cloud hampered operations and the observation of results. In combats Fighter Command destroyed 15 enemy aircraft, probably destroyed 4, and damaged 17. Our fighter losses were 17 aircraft and 16 pilots. Subject to the receipt of outstanding reports, our other losses are given as 20 bomber aircraft and 6 Swordfish.

(signed) J.B. Collier F/O

13th February,   Duty Intelligence Officer,
1942   HEADQUARTERS, FIGHTER COMMAND.

Author's note:

This official summary produced within 24 hours of the described events is, naturally, incomplete in final details and data. It is, nevertheless, remarkably accurate in regard to fighter pilots' claims for German aircraft destroyed in combat; an unusual occurrence. On the other hand the various claims by the Royal Navy and RAF Coastal Command to have struck certain German ships with torpedoes are patently optimistic. Perhaps the most significant points raised in this summary are the various occasions – mainly during the early stages of operations – when fighter escorts failed to rendezvous with the aircraft they were intended to protect and/or support.

Acknowledgments

Whilst accepting fully ultimate responsibility for all errors of fact or omission, and opinions – apart from those otherwise specifically indicated – within my text, I acknowledge readily and with deep gratitude the enormous help afforded voluntarily by so many people during my research and compilation. Foremost of these must be Eugene Esmonde's brothers, Owen, Witham and Patrick, and his sister Carmel. I am also indebted to the late Terence Robertson for use of his original research material, much of which appeared in semi-condensed form in his own account of the events of 12 February 1942, *Channel Dash* (Evans, 1958). Of the many others who so generously contributed reminiscences, records, photographs *et al*, I would particularly thank the following, listed alphabetically:

Captain R. Alderson, BOAC Retd; Squadron Leader J.A. Archer, RAF Retd; Captain R.G. Ballantine, BOAC Retd; R. Barker, Esq; J. Beedle, Esq; Captain W.W.R. Bentinck, OBE, RN Retd; Air Commodore I.E. Brodie, OBE, RAF Retd; J.W. Brooks, DFC, DFM; J.D. Brown, Esq; D.A. Bunce, CGM; Lt-Commander G.J. Cardew, RN Retd; Captain R.F. Caspareuthus, BOAC Retd; P.G. Cooksley, Esq; Air Commodore A.P.V. Daly, AFC, RAF Retd; Commander C.C. Ennever, DSC, RN Retd; E.R. Fawcus, Esq; Captain A. Foster, BOAC Retd; O. Garden, Esq; Rear Admiral P.D. Gick, CB, OBE, DSC, RN Retd; M.J. Gidman, Esq; Group Captain T.P. Gleave, CBE, RAF Retd; Mrs B. Gleeson; the late Captain H.L.M. Glover, BOAC Retd; G. Griffiths, Esq; Commander H.N.C. Hearn, RN Retd; Miss P. Houston; Father I Hulse, MBE, RN; D. Humphries, Esq; Squadron Leader W.A.K. Igoe, MRAES, RAF Retd; Lt-Commander C.M. Kingsmill, DSO, RNR Retd; Captain J.P. Kirton, BOAC Retd; Dr. A Korthal-Altes, LL.M; Commander

E.F. Lee, DSO, VRD, RNR Retd; J.H.A. Lewis, Esq; L.F. Lovell, Esq; R.V. Mitchell, Esq; Wing Commander L.S. Pegg, RAF Retd; Rear Admiral C.K. Roberts, DSO, RN Retd; Surgeon Rear Admiral R. Roberts, MD, RN Retd; B. Robertson, Esq; Lt-Commander R. McC Samples, DSO, RNR Retd;L.D. Sayer, Esq; H. Seymour, Esq; Lt-Commander G.H. Slade, RN Retd; P.C. Smith, Esq; Commander G.N.P. Stringer, DFC, RN Retd' R.C. Sturtivant, Esq; Mrs M. Main-Waddell; J. Winton, Esq; Squadron Leader A.L. Woode, AFC, RAF Retd.

In addition I received splendid co-operation and unfailing courtesy from the following sources; Fleet Air Arm Museum, Yeovilton; Imperial War Museum; Royal Navy Historical Division; Departments AR8b and OS9a of the Ministry of Defence; Public Records Office; *Chatham, Rochester, and Gillingham News*. I should emphasise here that such acknowledgements should not be read as implying official endorsement of my text necessarily, nor is the Ministry of Defence in any way responsible for any statements or conclusions expressed.

I would also like to thank Michael B. Yeats, Anne Yeats and Macmillan & Co for permission to quote from 'An Irish Airman Foresees his Death' by W.B. Yeats.

Select Bibliography

The Victoria Cross, 1856-1964, Sir J. Smyth; Muller, 1965
The VC & DSO, Creagh/Humphris; Standard, 1924
For Valour – The Air VCs, C. Bowyer; Kimber, 1978
Loss of the Bismarck, B. Scholefield; Ian Allan, 1972
The Cruise of the Bismarck, F. McMurtrie; Hutchinson, 1942
The Bismarck Episode, R. Grenfell; Faber & Faber, 1948
The Sinking of the Bismarck, W. Berthold; Longmans, 1958
Pursuit, L. Kennedy; Collins, 1974
The Story of the Prinz Eugen, F.O. Busch; R. Hale, 1956
Battleship Scharnhorst, Vulliez/Mordal; Hutchinson, 1958
The Loss of the Scharnhorst, A.J. Watts; Ian Allan, 1976
Escape of the Scharnhorst & Gneisenau, P. Kemp; Ian Allan, 1975
Channel Dash, T. Robertson; Evans, 1958
Fiasco, J.D. Potter; Heineman, 1970
Operation Thunderbolt, P. Cooksley; R. Hale, 1981
Bucknill Report, Admiralty (Command 6775), 1946
Fleet Air Arm, HMSO, 1943
The Fleet Air Arm, P. Kemp; H. Jenkins, 1954
Find, Fix, and Strike, T. Horsley; Eyre & Spottiswoode, 1943
Find, Fix, and Strike, J. Winton; Batsford, 1980
Wings of the Morning, I. Cameron; Hodder & Stoughton, 1962
Ark Royal, HMSO, 1942
Ark Royal, K. Poolman; Kimber, 1956
Ark Royal, W. Jameson; Hart Davies, 1957
Bring back my Stringbag, Lord Kilbracken; P. Davies, 1979
The Battle of the Atlantic, Costello/Hughes; Collins, 1977
Send her Victorious, M. Apps; Kimber, 1971
Victory at Sea, 1939-45, P. Kemp; Muller, 1957
Carrier operations in WW2, Vol 1, J.D. Brown; Ian Allan, 1968

The British Navy's Air Arm, O. Rutter; HMSO/Penguin, 1944
Swastika at Sea, C. Bekker; Kimber, 1953
The Luftwaffe War Diaries, C. Bekker; Macdonald, 1967
The First & the Last, A. Galland; Methuen, 1955
The Ship-Busters, R. Barker; Chatto & Windus, 1957
Fighter Command, P. Wykeham; Putnam, 1960
RAF Biggin Hill, G. Wallace; Putnam, 1957
43 Squadron, J. Beedle; Beaumont, 1966
Air War over Europe, 1939-45, C. Bowyer; Kimber, 1981
Air War against Germany & Italy, 1939-43, J. Herington; AWM, Canberra, 1954
Britain's Imperial Air Routes, R. Higham; Shoe String, 1960
Annals of British/Commonwealth Air Transport, J. Stroud; Putnam, 1962
Swordfish Special, W. Harrison; Ian Allan, 1977
History of RAF Manston, W. Fraser; Private, 1969
U-boats under the Swastika, J.P.M. Showell; Ian Allan, 1973
Years of Command, Douglas/Wright; Collins, 1966
Fairey aircraft since 1915, H.A. Taylor; Putnam, 1978
RAF 1939-45, Vol 1, D. Richards; HMSO, 1953
Night Strike from Malta, K. Poolman; Jane's, 1980
The Mighty Hood, E. Bradford; Hodder & Stoughton, 1959

Index

Index

The index of personal names is followed by a separate index of places on page 220
Names (Ranks contemporary)

Erratum: Kingcombe should read Kingcome CBF

Places